JERUSALEM
VISIONS OF RECONCILIATION

AN ISRAELI-PALESTINIAN DIALOGUE

Proceedings of the United Nations Department of
Public Information's Encounter for
Greek Journalists on the Question of Palestine,
27-28 April 1993, Athens, Greece

UNITED NATIONS

FOREWORD

At the request of the General Assembly of the United Nations, the Department of Public Information (DPI) carries out a special information programme on the question of Palestine. Included in this programme are a variety of projects, such as publishing books and booklets, holding fact-finding missions to the Middle East for journalists, and organizing "Encounters" between Middle East policy makers and analysts and members of the media from different countries and regions of the world.

On 27 and 28 April 1993, DPI convened an Encounter at Athens, Greece, to discuss the issue of the status of Jerusalem. The Encounter was supported by the Greek Government. The members of the panel were policy makers and analysts from Palestine and Israel, as well as from the Russian Federation and the United States of America. The participants were mainly representatives of the Greek media and non-governmental organizations. Also attending were foreign journalists based in Athens and the diplomatic corps.

It is hoped that readers can find in the discussions at the Athens Encounter useful insights into the many themes which relate to the question of the status of Jerusalem, and that this publication will contribute to Israeli-Palestinian reconciliation.

ATHENS ENCOUNTER: PARTICIPANTS

HOST COUNTRY REPRESENTATIVE

H.E. Mr. Michael Papaconstantinou
Minister for Foreign Affairs of Greece

MODERATOR

Mr. Mustapha Tlili
Chief, Anti-Apartheid, Decolonization and Palestine Programmes
Section, United Nations Department of Public Information

PANELLISTS

Dr. Albert Aghazarian
Director for Public Relations, Bir Zeit University
Ramallah, West Bank
Adviser to the Palestinian Negotiating Team

Mr. Moshe Amirav
Member of the City Council of Jerusalem

Ms. Yael Dayan
Member of the Israeli Knesset

Mr. Nicolas Galanopoulos
Counsellor of Embassy, Middle East Section
Ministry of Foreign Affairs of Greece

Ambassador Robert V. Keeley
President, The Middle East Institute
Washington, D.C.

Mr. Valery I. Kuzmin
Head, Israel and Palestine Section, Middle East Department
Ministry of Foreign Affairs of the Russian Federation

Dr. Ruth Lapidoth
Professor of International Law
The Hebrew University of Jerusalem

Dr. Sami Musallam
Director, Office of the Chairman of the Executive Committee
of the Palestine Liberation Organization (PLO)

Dr. Sari Nusseibeh
Member of the Steering Committee of the Palestinian
Negotiating Team, Jerusalem

Mr. Hanna Seniora
Publisher, *Al Fajr*
Jerusalem

Dr. Idith Zertal
Columnist, *Ha'aretz* Network, Tel Aviv

REPRESENTATIVES OF THE GREEK MEDIA

Mr. George Aidinis *	Athens Daily Newspaper Publishers' Association
Mr. Constantinos Angelakis *	Infogreece
Mr. George Angelopoulos	Ta Nea
Mr. Constantinos Argaliotis *	Epohi
Mr. Petrakis Athineos *	Eleftheri Ora
Ms. Natasa Bastea	Ta Nea
Mr. George Capopoulos	Kathimerini
Mr. Sofianos Chrysostomidis	Avghi
Ms. Evi Demiri	Greek Radio-Television
Mr. Panayotis Dizis *	ET-1 TV
Mr. Antonis Economides	To Vima
Mr. Stathis Efstathiadis	To Vima
Mr. Chris Eliou	Athens News Agency
Mr. Thanos Hatzopoulos	Niki
Mr. Michael Howard *	Greek News
Mr. Sotiris Kadinopoulos *	Ta Nea
Ms. Mirela Kalostypi	Era Radio
Ms. Maria Karchilaki *	Mega Channel TV
Ms. Thalia Kartalis	Kathimerini
Mr. Antonis Kassitas *	ET-1 TV
Mr. Leonidas Kondossis *	Thletora TV
Mr. Antonis Kondylas *	Mega Channel TV
Ms. Angeliki Konovesi *	Ena
Mr. Tassos Kostopoulos	Eleftherotypia
Ms. Nancy Kotrotsou *	Paron
Ms. Elpis Kotsaki	Athens News Agency
Mr. Takis Michas *	Kerdos
Mr. Ntinos Mitsis	Athens News
Mr. Mihalis Mitsos	Ta Nea
Mr. Mihalis Moronis	Eleftherotypia
Mr. Antonis Naxakis *	Avriani
Mr. Angelos Nezeritis *	Social and Economic Research
Ms. Irene Nicolopoulou	Mega Channel TV
Ms. Teta Papadopoulou	Anti
Mr. Antonis Papayannidis	Economicos
Mr. Mike Psillos *	Antenna TV
Mr. Nikos Sahas *	ET-1 TV
Mr. Gabriel Seretis	Antenna Radio
Mr. Dimitrios Stasinopoulos *	Panaitoliki
Ms. Marianna Tolia	Rizospastis
Ms. Olga Tremi	Flash Radio
Ms. Eleanna Tryfidou	Messimvrini
Mr. Krikor Tsakitzian *	ET-1 TV
Ms. Vicky Tsiorou *	Athens News Agency

* Observer

EXPERTS

Mr. Fragiski Abazopoulou	University of Thessaloniki
Mr. George Assonitis	Ionian University
Mr. Alexandros Cudsi	Institute of International Relations
Mr. Adamis Mitsotakis	Greek Institute of Defence and Foreign Policy
Mr. Constantinos Patelos	Panteion University
Mr. Efthymios Souloyannis	Academy of Athens
Mr. Charalambos Tsardanidis	Greek Institute of Defence and Foreign Policy
Mr. Stefanos Vallianatos	Greek Institute of Defence and Foreign Policy

REPRESENTATIVES OF NON-GOVERNMENTAL ORGANIZATIONS

Mr. D. Alhanatis	Jewish Community in Athens
Ms. Maria Gazi	Greek Committee for International Democratic Solidarity
Mr. Evanghelos Maheras	World Peace Council
Mr. Christos Marcopoulos	Movement for Peace, Human Rights and National Independence
Mr. Pericles Pangalos	Amnesty International/ Greek Section
Mr. Stelio Papadimitriou	Alexandros Onassis Foundation
Mr. Theoharis Papamargaris	Greek Committee for International Democratic Solidarity

REPRESENTATIVES OF POLITICAL PARTIES

Mr. Dimitris Stubos	Coalition of the Left and Progress
Mr. Panos Trigazis	Coalition of the Left and Progress

OBSERVERS

MINISTRY OF FOREIGN AFFAIRS OF GREECE

Mr. Panayis Cavallieratos	Counsellor of Embassy, Department of Religious Affairs
Ambassador Emmanuel Kalamidas	Head of the Middle East and North Africa Division
Mr. Panayotis Makris	Counsellor of Embassy, A5 Division
Mr. Elias Maltezos	Counsellor of Embassy, Head of A5 Communications Department
Mr. Nicholas Patakias	A5 Division
Ambassador a.h. Emmanuel Spyridakis	

DIPLOMATIC CORPS

Ambassador Abdullah Abdullah	Palestine
Mr. Muntaser Abu-Zaid	Counsellor, Palestine
Mr. Jorge Adrada	Chief, International Organization for Migration
Mr. Said Ahouga	Secretary, Morocco
Mr. Shawky Aly	Counsellor, Egypt
Ambassador Youssef Barkett	Tunisia
Ambassador Jean Cadet	France
Ambassador Christopher A. Edwards	Australia
Mr. Hassan Sherief El Sabban	Counsellor, Egypt
Ambassador Ahmed Nabil Elsalawy	Egypt
Ambassador José Fernandez	Philippines
Mr. Nigel Inkster	Counsellor, United Kingdom of Great Britain and Northern Ireland
Mr. Andreas Melan	First Secretary, Austria
Mr. Vassili Nassatis	Press Office, Saudi Arabia
Ambassador Valery D. Nikolayenko	Russian Federation
Ambassador John Noble	Canada
Mr. José Pombo	Minister-Counsellor, Uruguay
Mr. Valentin Poryazov	Second Secretary, Bulgaria
Mr. Luis Ramos	Secretary, Portugal
Mr. Ismat Sabri	Press Counsellor, Palestine
Apostolic Nuncio Luciano Storero	Holy See
Mr. Alberto Tamayo-Barrios	Chargé d'affaires, Peru

Ambassador Jan Valko	Slovakia
Mr. Bernhard Zobel	Press Counsellor, Germany

OTHERS

His Eminence *The Most Reverend Erineos*	Archbishop of Ierapolis, Exarch of the Holy Sepulchre in Greece
Ms. Ioanna Kourtovik	Lawyer
Ms. Christina Papadopoulou	Visiting Research Fellow, University of Cairo

FOREIGN CORRESPONDENTS

Mr. Sameh Abdallah	**Al-Ahram**
Ms. Athens Adams	**Allied Press International**
Mr. Moawif Ahmed	**Al-Arab/Al-Hayat**
Mr. Grahame Bennett	**Middle East Times**
Ms. Anthee Carassavas	**Voice of America**
Mr. Jean-José Cohen	**Radio Israel**
Ms. Ida-Maria Deuerling	**Neue Ruhr/Neue Rhein Zeitung**
Mr. Yannis Dimitriadis	**The Economist**
Mr. Louis Economopoulos	**Gulf Times (Qatar), NBC Radio**
Ms. Mercedes Gracia Aldde	**El Periódico de Catalunya**
Mr. Michael Howard	**Middle East Times**
Mr. Wesley Johnson	**Middle East International**
Mr. Nawab Khan	**Iranian News Agency**
Mr. Stefanos Kouteas	**Reuters Television**
Ms. Dina Kyriakidou	**Reuters**
Ms. Anne-Marie Ladoues	**Libération**
Mr. Li Cheng Gui	**Xinhua News Agency**
Mr. Vasilis Mousafiris	**Reuters**
Mr. Alain Navarro	**Agence France-Presse**
Mr. Aristotelis Sarricostas	**Associated Press**
Mr. Mansour Shashati	**Sudan News**
Mr. Panayotis Tsafaras	**Foreign Press Association**
Ms. Diana Tsoukatou	**Foreign Press Association**

SECRETARIAT

COORDINATOR
Mr. Robin Roosevelt
Information Officer, Anti-Apartheid, Decolonization and Palestine
Programmes Section, Department of Public Information of the
United Nations Secretariat

LIAISON OFFICER
Mr. Axel Wuestenhagen
Director
United Nations Information Centre, Athens

SECRETARY
Mr. Panayotis Karafotias
National Press Officer
United Nations Information Centre, Athens

PROGRAMME AND FEATURED SPEAKERS

INTRODUCTORY REMARKS

1

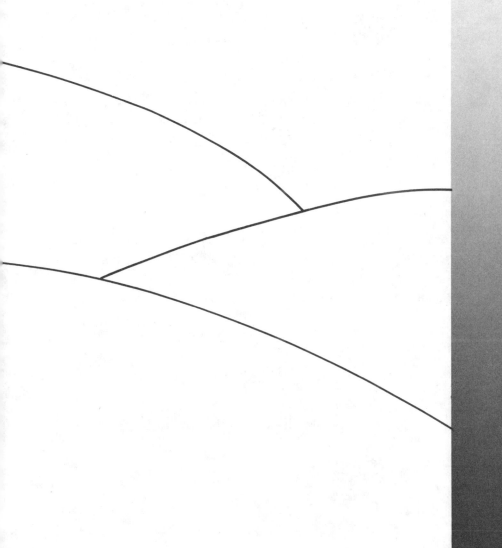

WELCOMING ADDRESS

H.E. Mr. Michael Papaconstantinou
Minister for Foreign Affairs of Greece

Today's Encounter, being held in Greece under the auspices of the United Nations, has a symbolic aspect, a symbolic meaning that transcends its essential contribution to advancing the peace efforts of the international community: it is the first specialized discussion concerning the present and the future of the city of Jerusalem. Participating in this discussion are representatives of all the parties involved. The fact that this Encounter is informal, without a strictly official character, and has been organized by the United Nations, makes the initiative even more interesting and attractive.

A few years ago it was thought that similar initiatives could be the prelude to organized negotiations towards the solution of the question of Palestine. Today this Encounter is being held as a follow-up to the already existing peace talks. The bilateral negotiations carried out between Israelis and Palestinians on the autonomy of the occupied territories could be a good starting-point for today's discussion. We in Greece hope that these discussions will be conducted in a positive and moderate atmosphere that will allow the consolidation of the viewpoints of each party.

The matter of Jerusalem cannot be considered outside the general framework of the situation in the Middle East. In the past the foundations were laid for the creation of a national Jewish homeland. Today it is generally understood that there is a need to create a national Palestinian homeland. We hope that the future will satisfy Palestinian expectations and at the same time reassure Israel. We sympathize with the moral dilemmas facing both parties. Greece has sacrificed a great deal on the altar of the fight for independence, but we also reached a time for dialogue and understanding. This country maintains friendly relations with Arab countries and Israel, and wants peace to prevail in the region. The policy of Greece on the Middle East issue has remained unaltered, regardless of the changes in Governments that have come into power from 1947 onwards. That year we saw the few remaining Greek Jews who had survived the German occupation of the country leave Greece and go to Palestine, where they started the fight for their national survival. But we never forgot that, for the Arab inhabitants, Palestine was the land of their forefathers. Finally, our stand was dictated by our belief in the principle of self-determination, which did not coincide with the idea that Palestine had to be partitioned. We hoped that the necessary regulations could be formulated so that Palestine would not be partitioned and at the same time the rights of the various communities could be guaranteed.

Today, obviously, with hindsight, we recognize that the non-application of the resolution that had been adopted by a majority in the General Assembly had tragic consequences. Among them, we lost the first chance to settle the question of Jerusalem in a way that would correspond to the common Jewish-Christian and Muslim heritage of the Holy City. The sensitivity of the Greek Orthodox Church on this matter is obvious. The Greek Orthodox Patriarchate of Jerusalem, which dates from the fourth century, has deep historic roots in that area. The nucleus is the Brotherhood of the Holy Sepulchre, formed largely by monks of Greek origin to host Byzantine emperors entrusted with guarding and preserving Christian places of worship. The legal status of the Patriarchate was consolidated with the Sultan's firman of 1852, which to this day is reinforced by international agreements and resolutions. The last major resolution is General Assembly resolution 181 (II) of 1947. The Greek Orthodox Patriarchate of Jerusalem is a purely religious organization that has no involvement in politics. In spite of that, the Patriarchate is undertaking an important task because, within its sphere of influence, it has managed to establish a harmonious relationship between the Greek, Arab and Jewish spirits, and to forge a bond of peaceful coexistence between the three religious communities.

The Greek position on the question of the Middle East is crystal clear: Palestinians cannot be deprived forever of their national homeland, but no settlement can be accepted if it does not guarantee the borders of Israel. Greece as a country, but also as a State member of the European Community, supports dialogue as the only possible solution to the problem. We believe that there is a need to continue peace talks with a view to finding a global, just and permanent settlement that will allow the countries of the area to live within safe borders. During the Greek presidency of the European Community in the first half of 1994, Greece will strive to contribute even more initiatives designed to bring the parties directly involved in the Arab-Israeli question closer together.

In closing, I should like to extend, on behalf of the Government and indeed the whole country of Greece, best wishes for great success in the work of this Encounter.

THE UNITED NATIONS PERSPECTIVE

Mr. Mustapha Tlili, Chief, Anti-Apartheid, Decolonization and Palestine Programmes Section, Department of Public Information of the United Nations Secretariat (Moderator)

When the question of Palestine was taken up by the United Nations in 1947, the United Nations Special Committee on Palestine was appointed by the General Assembly to present proposals on the issue. The Special Committee recommended in its report the partition of Palestine into an Arab State and a Jewish State and the territorial internationalization of the Jerusalem area as an international enclave in the Arab State in Palestine. Owing to the special status of Jerusalem, the Committee also unanimously recommended that the sanctity of the Holy Places be guaranteed by special provisions and that existing rights in Palestine be preserved.

On 29 November 1947, the General Assembly, in its resolution 181 (II), approved the Special Committee's recommendation. Often referred to as the partition resolution, resolution 181 (II) envisaged a demilitarized Jerusalem as a *corpus separatum* under the aegis of the Trusteeship Council of the United Nations, which could draft a statute for Jerusalem and appoint a governor. A legislature would be elected by universal adult suffrage. This statute would remain in force for 10 years and then be duly examined by the Trusteeship Council, with citizenship participation through a referendum. The Arab States rejected the resolution, declaring that the United Nations was exceeding its competence by proposing the partition of Palestine. The ensuing hostilities prevented the implementation of the resolution. Israel occupied the western sector of the Jerusalem area, destined for internationalization. Jordan occupied the eastern sector, including the walled Old City. Thus came into existence a de facto division of Jerusalem.

The General Assembly, however, by its resolution 194 (III) of 11 December 1948, reaffirmed both the principle of internationalization and existing rights. That resolution also contains far-reaching provisions for the wider Palestinian issue. The Arab States, refusing to recognize Israel, did not accept it. Israel also ignored the resolution and moved to extend its jurisdiction to that part of Jerusalem it had occupied. On 23 January 1950, Israel declared Jerusalem its capital and established government agencies in the western part of the city. The Government of Jordan, for its part, moved to formalize its control of the Old City; however, Jordanian legislation indicated that this action did not prejudice the final settlement of the Palestinian issue. I should mention here that on 31 July 1988, King Hussein made a declaration concerning the disengagement of Jordan's legal and administrative ties with the West Bank, occupied by Israel since 1967.

To return to the historical sequence, the de facto division of Jerusalem between two hostile States lasted until 1967. And as that division became protracted, two cities integrated into two hostile countries that progressively consolidated their existence as two separate worlds, an essentially Arab East Jerusalem and a Europeanized West Jerusalem. The war of June 1967 radically changed that situation. As a result of the war, Israel occupied East Jerusalem and the West Bank. Since then the status of Jerusalem has been put under extreme pressure by the occupying Power, and both the General Assembly and the Security Council in resolution after resolution have declared invalid the measures taken by Israel to change that status. Security Council resolution 252 (1968) in particular is very explicit in this regard. In paragraph 2, the Council considered ''that all legislative and administrative measures and actions taken by Israel, including expropriation of land and properties thereon, which tend to change the legal status of Jerusalem are invalid and cannot change that status''. And in paragraph 3, the Council urgently called upon Israel ''to rescind all such measures already taken and to desist forthwith from taking any further action which tends to change the status of Jerusalem''. The Security Council has reaffirmed these two positions numerous times. This was the case, for instance, in resolution 271 (1969) adopted by the Council following the outbreak of a major fire attributed to arson in August 1969 in Jerusalem's Al-Aqsa Mosque, one of the Holy Places of Islam.

Resolutions adopted during the 1970s, including those of the General Assembly, refer to the wider Middle East situation. Those resolutions are all based on Security Council resolution 242 (1967), which laid down the principles and provisions for a just and lasting peace in the Middle East. Among other things, the resolutions adopted since resolution 242 (1967) invariably reaffirm the established principle of the inadmissibility of the acquisition of territory by military conquest and express non-recognition of the Israeli occupation of East Jerusalem.

When steps were taken by Israel to make a united Jerusalem its capital, the Security Council on 30 June 1980 adopted resolution 476 (1980). After Israel's non-compliance with the resolution, the Security Council on 20 August adopted resolution 478 (1980), in which it reiterated its position that all actions altering the status of the city were null and void and called upon States that had established diplomatic missions at Jerusalem to withdraw such missions. The General Assembly also considered Israel's action to be a violation of international law which did not affect the continued application of the Fourth Geneva Convention [of 1949]. This understanding, affirmed in Assembly resolution 35/169 E of 15 December 1980, has been reaffirmed in subsequent years.

During the 1980s, United Nations resolutions dealt with the Jerusalem issue in the wider context of the inadmissibility of the acquisition of territory by force and the applicability of the Fourth Geneva Convention to the Palestinian territories occupied by Israel since 1967. As you can see, Jerusalem now is invariably included by both the General Assembly and the Security Council as part of the occupied territories.

More recently, as the international community and in particular the Security Council continued to follow with concern developments affecting the question of Palestine, two resolutions stand out as important actions of the Council. I refer first to resolution 672 (1990), adopted on 12 October 1990 following the violence which took place at Haram al-Sharif. The Council, after condemning "especially the acts of violence committed by the Israeli security forces resulting in injuries and loss of human life", called upon Israel, the occupying Power, "to abide scrupulously by its legal obligations and responsibilities under the Geneva Convention relative to the Protection of Civilian Persons in Time of War, of 12 August 1949, which is applicable to all the territories occupied by Israel since 1967".

The applicability of the Fourth Geneva Convention to Jerusalem as an occupied territory was again reaffirmed by the Security Council on 20 December 1990 in resolution 681 (1990), when it expressed grave concern at the deteriorating situation in "all the Palestinian territories occupied by Israel since 1967, including Jerusalem". The Council went on to urge "the Government of Israel to accept the *de jure* applicability of the Geneva Convention relative to the Protection of Civilian Persons in Time of War, of 12 August 1949, to all the territories occupied by Israel since 1967 and to abide scrupulously by the provisions of the Convention". The status of Jerusalem was thus again confirmed.

I have attempted to convey to you as clear and faithful a picture as possible of the United Nations position on the Jerusalem issue. However, notwithstanding the clarity of the position of the international community on the matter, I am reasonably certain that most of us here would agree that, of all the various aspects of the question of Palestine, the question of Jerusalem is perhaps the most difficult to address.

But then, isn't it even more imperative, both intellectually and morally, to devote more energy to solving problems considered to be more difficult? When different minds and minds of differing views, but luckily women and men of good will, get together, as we have here, that particular interactive effort in which these minds engage to tackle difficult issues is called dialogue—in a tradition that highly befits the great heritage of this great city of world civilization, Athens. Call then our Encounter a symposium, if you will, in homage to Plato, and to the people and the Government of Greece, our hosts, whom I wish to thank most sincerely, on behalf of the United Nations and the Secretary-General, for their support.

The purpose of this informal, day-and-a-half Encounter is to have an open and frank discussion on the difficult and complex question of Jerusalem. Together we will address such issues as sovereignty over the city, municipal responsibilities and tangible confidence-building measures that could lead to the reconciliation of the two parties, and we will do so within the overall context of international legality as embodied in United Nations resolutions and bearing in mind the aspirations of the two peoples, the Palestinian people and the Israeli people.

We have been fortunate to assemble for this dialogue a distinguished panel of policy makers, political analysts and media personalities from the two sides, as well as other highly qualified Middle East experts. Before I introduce them to you, let me make it clear that the titles, functions and other particulars associated with the names do not reflect a political position of the United Nations as far as Jerusalem is concerned. That being said for the record, it is my pleasure to introduce to you, in the order in which they appear on the programme, Ambassador Robert V. Keeley, President of the Middle East Institute in Washington, D.C.; Dr. Sami Musallam, Director of the Office of the Chairman of the Executive Committee of the Palestine Liberation Organization (PLO); Ms. Yael Dayan, Member of the Israel Knesset; Mr. Valery I. Kuzmin, Head of the Israel and Palestine Section in the Middle East Department of the Ministry of Foreign Affairs of the Russian Federation; Dr. Sari Nusseibeh, member of the Steering Committee of the Palestinian Negotiating Team, Jerusalem; Dr. Ruth Lapidoth, Professor of International Law at the Hebrew University of Jerusalem; Dr. Albert Aghazarian, Director for Public Relations at Bir Zeit University in Ramallah, West Bank, and Adviser to the Palestinian Negotiating Team; Mr. Moshe Amirav, member of the City Council of Jerusalem; Mr. Hanna Seniora, Publisher and Editor-in-Chief of *Al-Fajr* in Jerusalem; Dr. Idith Zertal, a columnist for the *Ha'aretz* Network in Israel; and Mr. Nicolas Galanopoulos, from the Ministry of Foreign Affairs of Greece.

Together with you, ladies and gentlemen of the Greek media, political experts and analysts, the members of the panel will explore creative approaches to the Jerusalem issue. This informal public dialogue under United Nations auspices is part of the ongoing efforts of the international community to find a solution to the question of Palestine. More specifically, it is part of the series of Encounters which the Department of Public Information of the United Nations Secretariat organizes every year at the request of the General Assembly to further the understanding of the question of Palestine in its various aspects. Without a doubt, Jerusalem is a major aspect of the question. Let us hope that together we will make a contribution to peace.

DIVERGENCES AND CONVERGENCES

2

PANEL

Ambassador Robert V. Keeley
Dr. Sami Musallam
Ms. Yael Dayan
Mr. Valery I. Kuzmin
Mr. Nicolas Galanopoulos

ROBERT V. KEELEY

In the time that has been allotted to me, 10 minutes, I shall not try to summarize contending positions on the question of Jerusalem nor lay out the different alternative solutions that have been proposed. I am sure that their proponents and opponents will have ample opportunity during this day and a half to present all possible views. But by way of introduction, I should like to make a number of observations, six altogether, that may help to establish a groundwork for the discussions to follow.

The first point is that this 4,000-year-old city of peace called Jerusalem is best known, among other things, for having been the city most often conquered by force of arms, more so than any other city of comparable age. At various stages it has been occupied or reoccupied by Canaanites, Jebusites, Jews, Babylonians, Assyrians, Persians, Romans, Byzantines, Arabs, Crusaders and Mamluks. Just in this twentieth century it has been ruled successively by Ottomans, by the British, by Jordanians and by Israelis.

Perhaps we should not allow ourselves to get too bogged down in history. The present time may be a unique opportunity to establish a permanent status for Jerusalem, as permanent as anything in history can be, and for the first time not by the force of arms but by negotiation, and with democratic approval by the city's inhabitants, which would also be a historical first.

Secondly, Jerusalem is not a separate issue but is part and parcel of the dispute that has lasted most of this century between the Israelis and the Palestinians, and the Jews and the Arabs in general, and it is, in fact, the most important bone of contention between the contending parties. This means that it cannot be dealt with in isolation or separately because it is central to a solution. It is all right to talk about the issue separately, as we will be doing today and tomorrow, but it cannot be settled separately.

The dispute over Jerusalem differs in degree but not in kind from the rest of the dispute. The sameness in kind lies in the recognition that the dispute arises from a struggle between two nations, peoples, ethnic groups, tribes, label them whatever you wish, over the same piece of territory. The difference in degree results from the emotional, religious and spiritual dimensions of Jerusalem—elements that are present in all disputes over land because of the peculiarly intense human attachment to the land of one's ancestors, but that are heightened in the case of Jerusalem because that land is considered holy by three religions.

My third point is that, because Jerusalem is considered such a difficult, complex and emotive issue the imperative to solve it has usually been relegated to the distant future, as something to be settled after all other issues have been resolved, as the final step to be taken in a comprehensive peace settlement. There is unlimited evidence for this fact and it is highlighted by the total absence of Jerusalem from the agendas being discussed in the [tenth round of the] peace talks, which are resuming today in Washington, D.C. Jerusalem is not even on the table. It was deliberately left out of the formula that was developed for the process that began [at the International Peace Conference on the Middle East] at Madrid, and it is to be taken up only in the final status talks to start three to five years down the road after the autonomy talks are successfully completed— that is, if they are successfully completed.

It is noteworthy that Jerusalem was left out of the Camp David accords, the only peace agreement reached thus far between Israel and its neighbouring States. Much is being made, and rightly so, of the presence for the first time on the official Palestinian delegation to the Washington talks of a resident of Jerusalem, Mr. Faisal Husseini, and most would agree that this is a positive step. But he will not be there talking about Jerusalem, at least not at this stage in the negotiations.

There are two points of view about this relegation of Jerusalem to the last item on the negotiating agenda. One is that, because the issue is so difficult, it would be better to settle easier matters first, and thereby build up some confidence and good will on both or all sides, after which conditions will be riper for tackling the problem of Jerusalem. Perhaps this view is also based on an unspoken belief that Jerusalem is nearly unsolvable, and therefore taking it up early on risks bogging down the negotiations in dead ends and blind alleys.

The opposite point of view, which I personally share, has been eloquently expressed by Cecilia Albin in a work that I shall cite again at the end of my remarks, as follows:

"Jerusalem is at the root of the larger conflict and combines all its essential elements including questions of legitimacy, mutual recognition and coexistence. The fact that the parties have not been able to agree on its future political status, and in some cases think that the issue is unresolvable, is a primary cause behind the persistence of the overall conflict. This being the case, confronting the Jerusalem issue early on may actually pave the way to a comprehensive settlement of the Arab-Israeli conflict. Efforts to actually determine in detail the permanent status of Jerusalem should in all likelihood be left to the final stage of a formal negotiating process. For these efforts to be successful, however, the necessary preparatory work must first have been completed, including joint exploration, discussion and evaluation of alternatives for a solution by the parties, and the implementation of a number of steps on the ground.''

Fourthly, while probably everyone agrees that the two parties which must come to an agreement on the status of Jerusalem are the Israelis and the Palestinians, who constitute the bulk of the population of the city, it is often overlooked in these discussions that the status of Jerusalem is of interest to vast numbers of people, billions in fact, around the world who are not direct participants in the conflict but who care deeply about how it is resolved in the specific case of Jerusalem.

There are, first of all, the millions of Jews who are not Israelis and never intend to be, but for whom Jerusalem is a spiritual embodiment as well as a symbol of the deepest significance. This extends even to secular Jews, for whom Jerusalem is the ethnic and cultural capital of their people, regardless of personal religious belief or practice.

Then there are the some one billion Muslims around the world for whom Jerusalem is also a holy city, the third most important in their religion, and this extends to an immense number of people who are neither Arabs nor inhabitants of the Near East region. If one doubts the importance of this factor, then one ignores the reactions around the world when an incident happens in Jerusalem that is deemed an affront to the Muslim religion.

Finally, there is the multitude of Christians for whom Jerusalem is also the primary Holy City and who under present conditions have a much lesser say in what will happen to the city than do their co-monotheistic believers of the Jewish and Muslim faiths. No doubt this explains why attempts to create an international status for Jerusalem have usually emanated from bodies where Christians dominate.

So we must recognize that Jerusalem is the city of David, and of Jesus and of Muhammad and of all their adherents around the world. The question is whether these outsiders should have a say in the final disposition of Jerusalem. My answer is ''yes'' and ''no''. ''No'', in that they should have no veto over a solution that is satisfactory to the inhabitants of the city—Jewish, Muslim and Christian. But ''yes'', in the sense that they should use their moral influence to encourage an outcome that will restore peace and harmony to this Holy City and terminate the state of conflict and war that has disturbed its peace. Needless to say, a necessary condition of any universally acceptable solution would be the guarantee of open and peaceful access to the holy sites of all religions for peoples of all faiths and nationalities without exception.

My fifth point is that there seems to be general agreement that the city should not be divided again, as it was from 1948 to 1967. A geographic division is likely to perpetuate conflict no matter how carefully it is worked out. This is underlined by the fact that, although the war of 1967 purportedly unified Jerusalem, the city remains today very divided in every sense that matters, intensely divided, troubled and unsafe. It could be argued that shared, dual or joint sovereignty over a unified city will make the city impossible to manage and govern and will perpetuate points of disagreement and conflict. While admitting this difficulty, I would argue that split sovereignty, or single sovereignty, would be much worse, in that such an outcome would be viewed by one or both sides as temporary and would encourage one or the other or both to continue the campaign to change this outcome. The losing party would be unlikely to accept the loss as permanent and continued conflict would be guaranteed.

My sixth and last point is that it is worth taking a backward look at the United Nations partition plan of 1947 embodied in General Assembly resolution 181 (II) and the part of it devoted to Jerusalem, which under that plan was to become an internationalized *corpus separatum*. I am not suggesting that that plan for the city is currently viable, as it appears to be unacceptable to both Israelis and Palestinians, but it has some merits as the only internationally sanctioned solution for the city. It has never been rescinded or repudiated, although no real efforts to bring it into being have been made at the United Nations or elsewhere since about 1952. But the plan deals with the problems of this special city in some interesting ways. The things that have been done to the city since 1947, including the annexation of the western part by Israel, the annexation of East Jerusalem by Jordan and the unification and annexation of the entire and large city by Israel after the war of 1967, have all gone unrecognized by the international community. I mention this as a reminder that a solution to the problem of Jerusalem which is acceptable to both the inhabitants and the international community would provide international legitimacy and recognition to a city that has lacked both for a couple of generations.

In conclusion, let me cite two studies that I have found im-
mensely valuable in preparing for this Encounter. One is a brief, and
therefore quite utilitarian, paper by Naomi Chazan that summarizes
the issues regarding Jerusalem in about 30 pages. It is entitled
"Negotiating the non-negotiable, Jerusalem in the framework of an
Israeli-Palestinian settlement", and it was published in the *Emerg-
ing Issues Series* of the American Academy of Arts and Sciences in
March 1991. The other document, as yet unpublished, is a much
longer work of some 235 pages. It is a doctoral dissertation which
Cecilia Albin has just recently completed and submitted to the Paul
H. Nitze School of Advanced International Studies of Johns Hopkins
University in Washington, D.C., and which I was permitted to borrow
and read. It is entitled "Resolving conflicts over indivisibles through
negotiations: the case of Jerusalem". This work includes a theoretical framework, as one would expect in a doctoral dissertation, a thorough examination of all the literature published to date, of which there
has been a great deal, a case-study of the Jerusalem conflict, the
author's own model for a solution—essentially a united city with dual
or shared sovereignty based on five core concepts—as well as a
strategy for bringing about negotiations. I hope that this work will
be published in due course, as it will be a valuable resource for anyone who must deal with this issue as we are trying to do today.

MODERATOR

We now have a picture of the positions of the two parties, but also
of the hopes on which the two parties can build to advance a solution of the question of Jerusalem. But before we discuss these hopes,
let me give the floor to Dr. Sami Musallam, Director of the Office
of the Chairman of the Palestine Liberation Organization, to state
the position of the Palestinians on the question of Jerusalem.

SAMI MUSALLAM

I might be able to state our position in less than 10 minutes because
the presentation Mr. Tlili made covered the United Nations aspect
of the issue, and Ambassador Keeley's summation of the problem
has helped to crystallize the issue, and so I am relieved of repeating
the same points. The title of this first panel discussion of our Encounter is "Divergences and Convergences", and the title of the Encounter is "Jerusalem: Visions of Reconciliation". I think that these terms
may be two sides of the same coin. To discuss the divergences, in

order to make convergences and to have or develop visions for the future of Jerusalem, the two peoples must find some creative solutions to a highly volatile issue which necessitates a strong will, and perhaps a stronger desire to offer confidence-building measures to the other party that could pave the road for developing creative visions for the future. Having said that, I should like to stress that the issue of Jerusalem for me is highly emotional because I come from Jerusalem. I was born there, lived there, was raised and educated there until 1967. My father lies dead there, lies in peace there. There are pictures that I never forget. For example, there is the picture that we saw immediately after the Six-Day War on 7 June 1967: General Moshe Dayan, who was then Minister of Defence, marching in triumph with his staff through St. Stephen's Gate and Babul-aspat in the direction of the Holy Al-Aqsa Mosque to pray at the Wailing Wall. The issue is also emotional because the question of Jerusalem for me represents the future of my children, one of whom was born in Beirut and the other in Tunisia, who don't know Jerusalem and don't know Palestine, but if you ask them where they are from, they will tell you immediately, "We are from Jerusalem".

The question of Jerusalem is, as Ambassador Keeley said, very important and central to three religions—Judaism, Christianity and Islam. Perhaps it is pertinent to point out here that the believers in the three religions will clash in Jerusalem, will disagree in Jerusalem or will make their peace in Jerusalem, and this will be paramount for future generations.

For Jews, Jerusalem is the Holy City that harbours the symbols of their faith.

For Muslims, Jerusalem is one of the three holiest cities in Islam, the bridge between the earthly world and paradise. It is the seat, in fact, of paradise where final judgement will take place. It is the first of the two kiblahs, and the third holiest shrine after the Kaaba in Mecca and the Mosque of Prophet Muhammad's tomb in Medina. It is the place of the ascension of Muhammad to heaven, what is called in Arabic *al-isra'*.

For Christians, and I am speaking as a Christian, Jerusalem is the message of Christianity as embodied in the crucifixion of Jesus Christ and his resurrection from death and the place of his ascension to heaven. So it represents the message of Christianity *per se*— namely, the redemption of mankind from original sin.

I turn now to more worldly issues. There is a problem in Jerusalem, and the problem for us Palestinians lies in the occupation of Jerusalem since 1967 by the Israeli forces. As Ambassador Keeley has already pointed out, occupation gives rise to a number of questions, such as the question of split sovereignty, of single sovereignty or shared sovereignty. Is Jerusalem part of the occupied territories conquered by Israel in the war of 1967 and does it thus come under the jurisdiction of Security Council resolution 242 (1967), which does not recognize the acquisition of territory by force? In other words, does a peace settlement apply to Jerusalem as well? Where are the frontiers of conciliation and compromise which can be made on the question of Jerusalem?

For us, Jerusalem has been declared the capital of the State of Palestine. In the Political Communiqué of the Palestine National Council accompanying the Declaration of Independence in Algiers of 15 November 1988, we stated our position that Jerusalem is part of the occupied territories conquered by Israel in 1967 from which the Israelis have to withdraw. In the present negotiations we have opted to defer discussing the issue to the later stages of negotiations in order to facilitate the progress of the negotiations on the general issue of conflict in Palestine—the national rights and the transfer of power from the occupation authorities to the Palestinian people. But the question of Jerusalem will always be there, hanging over the heads of all those participating in negotiations because they will have to address the issue in the final analysis.

Israeli policies since Jerusalem was occupied in 1967 have greatly complicated the question of Jerusalem. I will not discuss here all the policies that were adopted by the Israeli Government or by the municipality of West Jerusalem and imposed on East Jerusalem, because other panellists will be covering that, but suffice it to say that on 27 June 1967 Jerusalem was formally annexed to Israel. On that day the Knesset adopted a resolution that states that Israeli law and administration shall apply to all parts of Eretz Israel and that the Government shall act on these matters by decree. Since then all laws on Jerusalem have indeed been determined by decree. There have been quite a number of arbitrary measures, of plans, of schemes, made by the Government, or by the municipality of Jerusalem, changing the demographic character and original status of the city of Jerusalem, transforming it into what is termed the capital of Israel and destroying its Arab character. In this regard it is worth mentioning that there is a plan for Jerusalem, published on 23 January 1992 by the Israeli military magazine Ba-Maḥaneh, under the title "Jerusalem in the year 2000", which pinpoints the policies that the municipality of Jerusalem and the Government of Israel have for Jerusalem.

In this regard, I should like to say, for example, that the confiscation of land has been so extensive that when Israel occupied the eastern part of Jerusalem, i.e., the Old City and its environs and outskirts, the area of Jerusalem—which was only 15,000 dunums, approximately 1,500 hectares—was expanded to 60,000 dunums. And as

I just heard confirmed from our friends on the panel, they envision an area of 10 aerial miles for Jerusalem, which would extend from the northern limits of Ramallah to the southern boundaries of Bethlehem. There is a map of this plan. I do not know whether my colleagues will be circulating it to you or not, but it is available.

The problem that we face in Jerusalem is, as I said, the question of changing its demographic character and original natural status. The Israeli authorities have confiscated land, evicted people from their homes and from their land, demolished not only houses but, in fact, complete quarters, like the heart of the Magharibah in Jerusalem. That is the Magharibah Muslim quarter near Haram al-Sharif. There is a complete list of all these acts of desecration, confiscation and expansion at the expense of the Arab side. They can be discussed in negotiations or by other colleagues. But it is important to note that if we are looking for a solution to Jerusalem, these issues have to be addressed. The demographic character of the city has changed totally, especially as we know the Israeli Government has a plan to keep the Palestinian Arab population, whether Christian or Muslim, in Jerusalem to a level not exceeding 26 per cent of the total population of the city. This will, of course, affect any elections or referendums in the future on the final status of the city.

This Encounter is the first time the issue of Jerusalem has been handled within the United Nations context. Previous Encounters of the United Nations dealt with other aspects of the question of Palestine. Even though at this Encounter ideas may only be put on the table, and we may not agree on the premises or parameters of what should be done, I think it is a worthwhile exercise that has to be undertaken by people who have the courage to discuss this sensitive and complicated issue. We do not expect to arrive at solutions here, but if we are successful in portraying the problem, I think we will have had much success in our efforts.

YAEL DAYAN

I am really not going to speak about Jerusalem because, first, I believe that a solution to Jerusalem will be a result of a general peace settlement and, second, because my colleagues from Israel will be talking about the specifics dealing with that city.

I should like to comment on the fact that of all the very important and honourable representatives here, two are missing. We do not have an official representative of the United States Embassy, and we do not have an official of the Israeli Embassy. I would like to think that this is because they are very busy making peace in

Washington, D.C., not because they are avoiding discussions of peace in Athens.

I am going to speak differently now from the way I will later in this Encounter because I am altogether quite schizophrenic whenever it comes to peace. I used to be at ease when the Likud, the right wing, was in government. Then I would go from conference to conference and feel free to attack my Government because I was in the Opposition and my views were polarized. Now I am part of the Government and what I am going to present very briefly on the prospects of peace is really more about where the Israeli Government stands and more about the difference between this Government and the previous one, which people may fail to see because perhaps not enough evidence has been convincingly presented. Later, I shall speak about what I wish to happen. Now I shall try to make a few comments about what in fact is happening. I am very lucky that the peace talks are resuming in Washington today because if this Encounter had been held last week I would have been in a really difficult position.

Because the problem of Jerusalem is complex, because we are talking about a real chance for peace, I really believe it is not to avoid the subject that we are saying Jerusalem is not on the agenda now, which by the way does not prevent others from putting it on the agenda. We really believe that, once there is a framework for an interim arrangement that is acceptable to all sides, the question of Jerusalem will be tested during the self-rule period. During that period a few things will already be done concerning the population of East Jerusalem (not the territory of East Jerusalem) and I think that this is the only way to approach it. We should open the issue after two or three years' time, with an open mind, because certainly one would not find in any Israeli Government today a willingness to deal with the question of Jerusalem.

I want to make this very clear: no Israeli Government, be it Labour or left of Labour, certainly not anything that is centre or right of Labour, is going at this point to say anything other than that Jerusalem is the united capital of Israel, undividable and un-negotiable. This is something you are going to hear, and do not be misled by it. It does not mean that the Labour position is identical to the previous Likud position. It does mean that this Government is going to separate the status of the East Jerusalem Palestinians from the status of the actual land that was annexed.

I should like to make a few remarks about the differences between the present Government and the previous one, and perhaps make some comments in a very blunt way.

We have heard about the good intentions of the United Nations and the very important decisions it has taken during the past 45 years. I do not want Mr. Tlili to be disappointed and I do not want anyone who is supportive of the cause of peace on behalf of the United Nations to be disappointed. But we are old-timers in world politics and I can say one thing: the United Nations is not going to deliver Palestine to the Palestinians. The United States of America is not going to deliver Palestine to the Palestinians. Saddam Hussein and anyone who promised the Palestinians a State by the use of power and the use of military force is not going to deliver a Palestine to the Palestinians. The United States, the might of the Soviet Union remaining in the Russian Federation of today, the great Powers of the world, the great armies of the world, any army that has connections with terrorist acts of any kind, any degree of terrorism, none of them are going to deliver a Palestine to the Palestinians within whatever borders. The only force, the only authority, the only country in the world that is going eventually, whether it wants to or not or is enthusiastic about it or not, to come to a deal that will make possible Palestinian independence is the State of Israel.

This does not mean that the United Nations is not important, although decisions will be taken, and have been taken, that try to prevent many Israeli actions, but they were not successful. It does not mean that the United States, one Administration or another, is not going to exert so-called pressure on Israel. It does not mean that the Russian Federation will not try to exert pressure, but one thing should be made clear and I think that deep inside the Palestinians know it very well: the one and only solution to the Palestinian question in the sense of a solution to the Israeli-Palestinian, Israeli-Arab conflict lies in the hands of the State of Israel, the Government of Israel, and because we are a total democracy, in the hands of the people of Israel.

I am not an egomaniac, and I am not saying, ''Look at us, we have a nuclear option, we have the strongest army in the Middle East and this is why the solution lies in our hands.'' The solution to the conflict is in our hands because Israel needs peace and needs a solution. Israel is not doing a favour to the Palestinians by eventually withdrawing, by going into an interim arrangement and by eventually making possible Palestinian independence and repartition of the area between the Mediterranean and the Jordan. We do not regard it, even the right wing does not regard it, as some kind of favour. There is no possibility that Palestine will be erected and founded by power, and yet Israel knows that there is no way to prevent a Palestine by the use of power. And for Israel, for its people, for its State, for its collective memory and historical prospects, the need for peace is not in the sense that we will do a favour and get the best conditions we can; rather peace is possible and the Israeli peace and the Israeli concept of peace is possible because we know that unless we live in coexistence, unless the occupation stops, unless we are equal peoples, whether it is a two-State situation or a confederation between the Palestinians and Jordan with Israel as a separate entity, or an Israeli-Palestinian-Jordanian confederation, whatever form the separation, the independence of the Palestinian people takes, we are really more than Siamese twins. There will not be an Israel which will fulfil our dreams unless there is a Palestine which fulfils the dream of my Palestinian colleagues here.

So it is purely for selfish and national Israeli reasons that people like myself and the present Government are trying to advance towards a solution, with the knowledge that there will not be a solution unless there is a compromise. I mean a proper territorial compromise, a repartition of the area, new borders and equality between the Israeli people and the Palestinian people and, I hope, mutual recognition in taking complete care of the security of the State of Israel because there are no risks that can be left unattended.

I should like to say that whoever thinks, and I have heard it from Chairman [Yasser] Arafat [of the Palestine Liberation Organization] and from many Palestinian colleagues in the heat of argument, that there is no difference between [Prime Ministers Yitzhak] Shamir and [Yitzhak] Rabin is wrong. They cite, and rightfully so because it was a disastrous decision, the deportation. They cite the very tough human rights situation and the violence in the occupied territories. But I should like very briefly to state the differences between Mr. Rabin and Mr. Shamir.

The previous Government did not, and I repeat and underline, *did not*, have any intention of carrying out any part of the Madrid framework. The previous Government regarded autonomy, full stop, as its definitive solution to the Palestinian people. No division, no recognition, no withdrawal. The bottom line of all the discussions we are having now—where the border will be, what the elements of the interim arrangement will be—is that we, Palestinians and the Israeli Labour-led Government, share what was not shared by the previous Government. We are talking about [Security Council] resolution 242 (1967), very clearly. We are talking about resolution 242 (1967) for the final, definitive solution. We are talking about resolution 242 (1967) for all the territories. We are talking withdrawal; we are saying the word "withdrawal". The Israel Army, the State of Israel, will not be sovereign over the Palestinian people within whatever borders are decided on. This is being said loud and clear. It will be said this week in Washington. This linkage with resolution 242 (1967), as it is implied in fact, will be the factor in the definitive arrangement, and it is going to be a guideline in the interim arrangement. This is something that was not made clear, not clear enough, by Mr. Rabin. But what was made clear by Mr. Shamir in the previous Government was that there was no intent whatsoever to have any Arab sovereignty over the occupied territories, or, as they used to call them, Judea, Samaria and the Gaza Strip.

We are back to "West Bank". We are back to "occupied territories". We are back to absolute determination to end the occupation. These are not similarities between Mr. Shamir and Mr. Rabin. This is a commitment of the present Government, and unless it fulfils this commitment, the present Government will not last and we will be into the next war, because opposition in the street is still very, very strong. And I want to make a comment here which is really about a failure on our part. We did win the elections. It was a revolutionary victory. The Likud is over. The right wing is down after 15 years. But we must not deceive ourselves. We won by a very small majority. The majority of the people of Israel are not for a two-State solution. They accept the interim. They know we will withdraw. They voted for resolution 242 (1967) and they will carry it out. But do not underestimate the Israeli Opposition. Do not underestimate the terrible fears of the population of Israel. Do not underestimate the effect of terror and Muslim fundamentalism. Hopefully, we will be able to show achievements on this common denominator of eventual separation, withdrawal and equality before the next elections, while at the same time terror is being reduced in one way or another.

If [the] Labour [Party], if Mr. Rabin does not do it, nobody will. This is one thing I have to give him credit for. I am on his back and I have had arguments with him. I think he should go faster and more openly, and I think Israel is strong enough and should make not gestures but peace in a much faster and more generous way. I think Israel can afford it. I think it has the support of the world for it. I think the Israeli population can afford it. But Israel cannot seem to bring itself to fight terror and immediately after, at the same time, make concessions with an easy heart, feeling that they are not political concessions but concessions on people's security.

We have got a very short time—three years. If we do not make it in these three years, it will not be [the] Labour [Party], it will be Ariel Sharon. It will be the right wing. It will be again back to a greater Israel notion. Do not let us all, Palestinians and Israeli peace camp people, deceive ourselves.

To Mr. Tlili I say, with all due respect, that the United Nations will not give the Israelis and the Palestinians the peace they need. The United States, Mr. Keeley, which is absent here officially, and the

Arab world will not give Palestine and Israel the peace they need. So let us in the next three years take a lot of short cuts. Because one thing I can promise you, and this is the difference between the present Government and the last one: this Government means peace with withdrawal. It means territorial repartition. If you do not accept this, we will waste time, since we have all agreed that the interim arrangement will lead to these things. If we waste time, before we know it there will again be another 10 or 15 years of another Government that we will not be able to do anything about, with all due respect to United Nations decisions and the others.

As the negotiations are being resumed in Washington, D.C., I should like to say what I have said to Chairman Arafat and to Prime Minister Rabin: one needs proof. This is imperative because Chairman Arafat said to me, "I don't see the difference between Rabin and Shamir. I know there is a difference but I need proof for my people to show them the difference and the sooner the better if I want to remain a majority in my street." I think that as of today there are a number of proofs, and I do not call them gestures because I refuse to deal with human rights in the terminology of gestures. Human rights are not a gesture; they are a must. Human rights are not a favour; they are to be taken for granted—the right to receive them and the duty to give them. The resumption of the peace talks today in Washington, D.C., is based on a quicker, much quicker, solution to the problem of the deportees. As I said before, the deportation was a disastrous decision and, other than being stupid, in my mind it was immoral and illegal.

The resumption of the talks is also based on acknowledging East Jerusalem rights and primarily adding Mr. Faisal Husseini to the delegation, and accepting that fully. The talks go into a phase where there will be deportees returning. The problem of administering the State land in the occupied territories will undergo tremendous change. And all these are understandings before the talks. There is an understanding which is a principal one, that resolution 242 (1967) is serving as a linkage and guideline towards the definitive solution, although it will not be implemented in the sense of withdrawal in the interim solution. But a serious redeployment of the army is going to be implemented. I hope we are going into quick elections in the territories so there is a reconfirmation of their official leadership. There is a very lenient position taken towards the PLO outside Israel. Certainly it will be involved fully when we come to negotiate the definite solution. It is involved by proxy, but much more than that when we are discussing the interim solution. We have cancelled the law which prohibited meetings with the PLO, so while I would be sitting here in any case, even if that law had not been cancelled—and I am sure that my Palestinian friends would have supplied my jail cell with oranges or dates from Tunis—it was a very important decision that was taken immediately by this new Israeli Government and Parliament. We are trying to remove all obstacles of that nature.

We have stopped, for all practical purposes, the building and construction of new settlements, as well as the financial incentives. I know it is not satisfactory to the Palestinians because there is still some building being completed. But all financial benefits that were directed to the occupied territories, to the settlers, have stopped. At the same time, we are not only encouraging the entry of, but channelling, big sums of money into the territories. It is not Israeli State money, it is Palestinian tax money and European money channelled hopefully into infrastructural work. And we are not waiting until the autonomy begins. It is not lip-service. It has to be done and the sooner the better. Washington should not delay. And all these things, as I mentioned, offer immediate proof of the differences between Mr. Rabin and Mr. Shamir, of the differences between Yael Dayan and Benjamin Netanyahu. I think that this coming round of talks will produce a completely different atmosphere. A lot of it depends on people like ourselves who are sitting here trying perhaps to accelerate their own speed and push their own Governments and authorities in order to move beyond many obstacles so that the people of Israel, the people of Palestine, can begin to see the results not in terms of the price of peace, but in terms of the advantages, the gains of peace.

MODERATOR

Ms. Dayan raised the question of the absence of the United States Ambassador and of the Israeli Ambassador. I can assure her that both of them were invited, but it is of course their sovereign decision to accept or not to accept the invitation.

YAEL DAYAN

It does not have to be an ambassador. I would be satisfied with someone of any level. This is the first conference ever—and we have been to many sponsored by the United Nations—which has the blessing of the Ministry of Foreign Affairs of Israel. Before, we were really boycotted whenever we came to a town to meet with Palestinians. This Encounter—our participation, our meeting with Palestinians, including Tunis Palestinians—has the official blessing of the Foreign Ministry of Israel. Our participation is not illegal any more, and this is a most welcome development. I hope that in these two days we may have a visit from the Israeli and American Embassies.

VALERY I. KUZMIN

It is a great honour for me to take part in such a representative Encounter, which, for the first time, aims to look into such a complicated issue. For us Russians, not only for the Orthodox Christians but for the people as a whole, Palestine and Jerusalem mean a lot. It is enough to mention the fact that, not far from Moscow, there is a small town called New Jerusalem. It is well known for its churches and monasteries, and this shows the degree of affection and the multitude of ties which bind us with the land of Palestine and with Jerusalem itself.

But nowadays, while approaching this issue, we must clearly bear in mind the fact that it cannot be divorced from the general ongoing peace process. It is not only a happy coincidence that today we have got together at almost the same moment that the bilateral peace negotiations are resuming in Washington, D.C.; it is also an incentive for us to look into this issue, which is left off the agenda, as has been mentioned by previous speakers.

Putting aside the official position of our country, which is, I suppose, well known to you, I must say that it is my personal deep belief and conviction that only by pursuing the way of the peace process that is now going on can we facilitate the settlement of, or any kind of solution to, the Jerusalem issue. For the first time in history, positive and favourable circumstances have been created, though the process is constantly interrupted by hindrances and obstacles appearing on the ground. Still this atmosphere is now more favourable than ever before. The basic thing that should be applied during this process is, to my mind, the principle of a compromise solution, mutually acceptable to both parties, and some sort of application of the well-known formula, land for peace.

I believe that only a successful continuation of the peace process will pave the way for any practical undertaking on Jerusalem, because of the sensitivity and diverse controversial interests involved in this issue. Otherwise, I am afraid we will be doomed to another cycle of violence with an unpredictable outcome. It is important that our discussions here be constructive and positive, preserving that fragile balance of mutual understanding which permitted the peace process to start and now to resume. Too many dangers are still there and we should avoid them.

My perception of the issue is based upon the assumption that any practical process, any principal agreement between the main parties involved—the Palestinians and the Israelis—allows for the active role of the international community, maybe not formally through the United Nations, but through the international community of the hundreds of millions of believers already mentioned by the speakers in today's Encounter.

Most importantly, I would emphasize the point that in my opinion any solution to the issue of Jerusalem will inevitably be of a compromise nature. Neither side can afford to impose its own position, its own vision of the settlement, on the other side, in good measure because of the disastrous psychological and moral effect that it would have on its own morale and its own, if you like, ideological or political underpinnings.

The historical background should be taken into consideration, and the main item that I shall dwell on is the fact that the Jerusalem issue has a very heterogeneous religious and cultural nature which cannot be avoided in any deliberations on the conflict and in any settlement of this issue. In my opinion, we cannot avoid mentioning United Nations legality, or United Nations resolutions, which create the legal basis for further deliberations. In that regard, the United Nations decisions stem from the assumption that there should be a specific, not traditional, status of Jerusalem as the Holy City for three world religions. They also stem from the city having been once divided, while claimed by the two parties to the conflict in Palestine.

Now that we are facing the problem of encouraging and facilitating the peace process, maybe not enough importance is given to such aspects as providing for better understanding, mutual respect and trust, creating a better atmosphere around the process. In this regard, I should like to dare to propose several things, confidence-building measures, directly relating to the Jerusalem question, though of course I understand that the issue is not on the agenda of the negotiations of the peace process itself. Maybe such suggestions can be taken into consideration by the parties, not formally, but in the general spirit of their intention.

First of all, I should like to propose that we think about the possibility of renouncing any further changes in the demographic character of the city, at least for a limited grace period during the negotiations which we are facing now. On the other hand, it should be balanced by the renunciation of, or at least abstention from, violence so as to normalize the atmosphere of the intercommunal relations in the city itself.

There are several issues of a humanitarian character that were addressed in part by Ms. Yael Dayan. I should like to mention, among them, some things that can be done even at the present stage of the peace process: family reunification, minimizing administrative restrictions for the Arab residents of Jerusalem, and participation of the residents of East Jerusalem in future elections and a greater and fairer share for them in the management of the municipal affairs of the city where they live. For the negotiators, and for us maybe, it would be useful to look into such matters as the formal engagement of the Arab population, the residents of East Jerusalem, in the exercise of municipal power.

NICOLAS GALANOPOULOS

In the light of the remarks of the previous speakers, I should like to make a few short comments. None of the issues under discussion today are simple. However, these exploratory talks can lead to a better understanding of each other's positions. We cannot easily reverse the course of history. Solutions that were applicable in the past are inapplicable now. However, Jerusalem in the minds of Greeks is associated with the most sacred shrines of Christendom. I hope the discussions will help the journalist-participants in the discussions to arrive at a better understanding of the Palestinian problem and its connections with the issue of Jerusalem.

The principles throughout the current peace process in the Middle East originated in Madrid in October 1991 and still remain unchanged. These principles are Security Council resolutions 242 (1967) and 338 (1973); the principle of land for peace; the right of all States in the region, including Israel, to live within secure and recognized boundaries; and the proper expression of the right of self-determination of the Palestinian people. These principles also apply in the case of Jerusalem.

East Jerusalem is a territory that Israel occupied in 1967. Settlement activity in the occupied territories is threatening the demographic status of Jerusalem. The international community cannot remain indifferent to any attempt to change that status. We hope that the Rabin Government will stick to its original promises not to encourage the building of settlements in Jerusalem, which are illegal under international law.

We can never recognize the occupation of Palestinian land, in the same way as we never recognized seizure of foreign land elsewhere. We did not recognize the Jordanian occupation of East Jerusalem in 1948 and we never recognized the Israeli occupation of East Jerusalem in 1967.

Ms. Dayan spoke about the necessity of new frontiers for the Palestinian State, which is to be a point of discussion in the talks. From our point of view, we would like to note that a strategic argument cannot be the obstacle to the fulfilment of the aspirations of another people. An example of Israel's strategic argument is the short distance between the town of Netanya and the Mediterranean Sea, and I remind you that Netanya was the old frontier of Israel from 1948 until 1967. I give you an example of the same, an analogous case in Greece. The northern frontier between Greece and Bulgaria is 20 kilometres from the Aegean Sea. But that has never been used as a strategic argument to put up an obstacle to the creation of friendly relations between the two countries. Respect for international law should be the foundation for relations between neighbouring countries.

FLOOR DISCUSSION

Mr. Ntinos Mitsis
Ms. Yael Dayan
Mr. Mihalis Moronis
Dr. Albert Aghazarian
Moderator
Mr. Pericles Pagalos

Dr. Sami Musallam
Dr. Sari Nusseibeh
Mr. Evangelos Maheras
Mr. Moshe Amirav
Mr. Tassos Kostopoulos

NTINOS MITSIS (Athens News)

I should like to put two questions to Ms. Dayan. First, you said, Ms. Dayan, that the Labour Government in Israel is willing to discuss all things concerning the borders and the withdrawal of the occupying army. Your position seems to be that this occupation has to end. My question is whether your opinion or the opinion of the Government of today in Israel includes considering withdrawal all the way back to the borders existing before the Six-Day War. A second question: you said, if I understood correctly, that all Governments in Israel have considered Jerusalem as the non-negotiable capital of Israel. If this is the position of the Government, then my question is: What would be the meaning of the negotiations being held in Washington when they reach the point of discussing the subject of Jerusalem?

YAEL DAYAN

The present Israeli Government is not talking about going back to the exact 1967 borders. We are talking about minor border correc-tions, having mostly to do with defence arrangements. We are talk-ing also about defence arrangements which will be for an interim period that will have nothing to do with the international borders, such as demilitarization of the West Bank and Gaza. Although I am not talking now about the Golan, the same applies really to all the borders, and we are equally concerned with a topic that is not to-day's topic, namely, the peace talks with Syria. On both fronts, the Syrian and the Palestinian, and in both areas, Gaza and the West Bank, we are not talking about returning to the 1967 borders, but about a variety of border corrections. Exactly where the line will be is subject to negotiations. I am sure that any Israeli Government will try to drive a hard bargain on security issues and will try to exclude from Israel as many Palestinians as possible. That is why when we talk about the Gaza Strip, where there isn't really a geographical security problem but there is a massive population, we are talking in terms of the Gaza Strip in its entirety. When we talk about the West Bank, we are talking about a few border corrections to comply with security needs. When the formulation of [Security Council] resolution 242 (1967) was being debated, there was a big argument about whether to call it withdrawal from the territories occupied in 1967 or, as was finally accepted, withdrawal from territories. In other words, even resolution 242 (1967) does not apply to all the territories. Of course, I hope the key will be to make the area that we withdraw from not only viable but with a very logical and decent continuity, not to turn it into a patchwork. There will be a question of how to connect the Gaza Strip and the West Bank. So when we say minor border corrections, that certainly does not imply a return to the 1967 borders.

There is a variety of opinions. The point is not to draw maps until we talk about the definitive solution. And I think this is wise because we have settlers in the West Bank. We foresee the dismantling of the settlements or at least offering the settlers the possibility of continuing to be where they are but under Arab sovereignty and not under Israeli sovereignty. It is an internal Israeli problem, but it is a very serious one which we do not want to raise as an issue now and create an impossible situation. As I said, all these are subject to negotiation, but to answer your question directly—no. We are going to withdraw from territories but not from *the* territories.

As to discussing Jerusalem, that is again a two-stage thing. It was discussed even at Camp David. The question of Jerusalem came up at Camp David and it was resolved by preparing bilateral letters from [President Jimmy] Carter to [President Anwar] Sadat and a separate one from [President] Carter to [Prime Minister Menachem] Begin. So there was not really an understanding, and yet there was an understanding as to where each of the sides stands. I think in the interim arrangement, when we talk about the autonomy, which is what is being discussed now in Washington, the population of East Jerusalem, not Jerusalem, will be offered a solution. We feel that it is our responsibility not to exclude the Palestinians of East Jerusalem from any kind of decision-making about the future of their political entity. It does not mean that East Jerusalem is going to be a part of the autonomy. There is no question in my mind that if this at any point is to be a precondition, nothing will move. So the first stage is really making sure that the East Jerusalemites participate fully in whatever is offered as an interim arrangement and self-rule in the territories, other than the annexed Jerusalem as a territory. It is only at the next stage that Jerusalem will have to be discussed in practical terms, and I hope by then our imagination will work overtime in order to provide more than a black and white, either/or solution. I am sure that we will find some things completely un-negotiable, on the one hand, and a possible solution by which Jerusalem would be the capital of Palestine, independent Palestine, on the other. It may require another interim phase just for the Jerusalem question after the autonomy, another interim phase just in order to reach an agreement on Jerusalem. The way it is now, Washington has got a full agenda and it is not discussing Jerusalem. It is not discussing a definitive solution. It is not discussing Palestine or the capital of Palestine. It is promising it in the sense of resolution 242 (1967) and nothing more.

MIHALIS MORONIS *(Eleftherotypia)*

I have a question for Ms. Dayan. She raised a subject that in the past years has taken on quite a dimension, and that is the matter of Islamic fundamentalism in the occupied territories. One of the causes can be found in the recent policy of the Israeli Government. Although 18 months have elapsed since the negotiations started, we do not see any concrete solution. Now, since the matter was raised by Ms. Dayan, does she foresee that the Government of Israel will face this problem through some specific results in the negotiations, or does she even see the possibility that the Palestine Liberation Organization will be recognized?

YAEL DAYAN

This is really a question which is like six different questions. I shall try to put them together. As for fundamentalism, I would really refer the question to my Palestinian colleagues more than to Israel. As I have said previously, Israel has made the mistake—and Mr. Rabin added to it by the deportation—of really strengthening the Hamas and the [Islamic] Jihad fundamentalist organizations in Israel with the very doubtful intent held by the previous Government of weakening the PLO by strengthening the fundamentalists. This was a terrible mistake and it is a mistake that really resulted from the desire to create a feeling in the Israeli public that all Arabs are alike, that they are all murderers, that they are all against a peaceful solution. There was never any recognition by the Shamir Government that there is a huge difference, namely, that one group has got on its agenda the destruction of the State of Israel while a majority of the Palestinian people in Israel and outside of Israel have accepted for all purposes the existence of the State of Israel and are going to accept a solution that is not all or nothing, but a compromise solution. It is still not clear to a lot of Israelis, I must say. The terror is mixed—there is fundamentalist terror as well as PLO-sponsored terror—and I'm not laying blame, it's just a fact: most Israelis still think of the PLO as an organization that calls in its [National] Charter for the destruction of the State of Israel. I know all the answers to this on my level. I know what [Chairman Yasser] Arafat says to me. But the man on the street has not heard it from Mr. Arafat or from anybody else. He hears from his own Government, and he hears from Palestinians, that the call for the destruction of Israel is still in the [Palestine National] Charter. He does not have the trust to believe that the real purpose of the Palestinian people is not the destruction of the State of Israel. There isn't a distinction, a sufficient distinction, between fundamentalist Palestinians and peace-seeking, peace-with-compromise-seeking Palestinians. That is something we should be working on together. I do not think it will happen through a government statement. This has to be really brought into people's minds and it will have to be done in a very serious way. One of the ways, of course, is the cessation of terror. I am not speaking about the *intifadah*. I am talking about terror proper against Jews because they are Jews, against civilians and within the borders of Israel.

In general, and I would like to hear a Palestinian comment on this, Muslim fundamentalism is really not an Israeli problem. It is an Arab problem just as much as it is an Israeli problem and you do not need refugee camps to create it, although they do contribute to it, certainly. You have got it in Egypt. You have got it in countries where it stems from students, even from groups that are well-to-do. The easy way to connect squalor, poverty, oppression and occupation is to say that this is the background for fundamentalism. Unfortunately this is not quite the case. Fundamentalism was produced in different nurturing grounds and we have to combat it together. Not by the deportation of Hamas adherents. It is a world problem. It is a Middle East problem and I think that this is one of the purposes for which we have to come together. This will be one of the tasks of Palestinian society once it has its self-rule, and before it is totally independent. Palestinians will have to handle it, and I should like to hear how they are going to do so. I think it will have to happen mostly on a societal level, on social and spiritual levels. They will have to make it worth while to be a proud Muslim or a proud Palestinian, without having to resort to the help of God or the help of terror. And I am sure that they will be successful in this, and the sooner they apply themselves, and are given the means to apply themselves to it, the better.

As for 18 months having gone by with nothing happening, my count does not begin 18 months ago. Madrid set a certain framework that, by the way, I personally think is a wrong framework. I think that it is wrong to sort of turn it into something holy. It has got a lot of flaws which were made in the beginning to accommodate Mr. Shamir, who did not want the peace that we are talking about. Therefore, I am not talking 18 months. I am counting the last, really just one, round of talks at the end of which some advances were made. The deportations certainly, together with the American elections, by general agreement, postponed things. But with the deportations, especially, we lost a lot of time and they cost us a lot of lives, and this was a very grave mistake and it caused a very grave delay.

I have a feeling that the real countdown begins today. We have been sending feelers towards each other, both sides, when we had the last round of talks. But we still had a Likud ambassador in the United States and we had the old framework. I think that the Madrid framework is broken now, a little bit, although not sufficiently for my taste. The association of the United States is going to be different this time. Let us begin a new countdown with the understanding that 18 months were not totally wasted (but almost), let us begin a new countdown now with an obligation to speed it up and make up for time lost.

I am very optimistic about this next round, simply because of the sense of total urgency. The situation is terrible in the territories. Again, I do not like to call this a human rights issue. It is just that living conditions in every possible domain are terrible. Terror in Israel has reached a height which makes it impossible for the Government to function the way it wants to function. There is a great urgency to pull together and start showing both our peoples that, yes, there is hope. Yes, there is a chance. Yes, there is a light at the end of the tunnel. I think that this round is going to do it.

MODERATOR

Ms. Dayan has mentioned some aspects of the problem that could be addressed by our Palestinian colleagues. I give the floor for that purpose to Dr. Aghazarian.

ALBERT AGHAZARIAN

I think that Ms. Dayan really reflects some of the complexities of the problem. It is clear that she reflects the opinion of a broad spectrum of Israelis and not just the Labour Party—the attitude, for example, that the United Nations does not count; the attitude that even the

United States Administration does not count; that in the final analysis it is only Israel that counts, and that Israel's motivation in the negotiations is not its love for Palestinians, but the self-interest of Israel. I think that this summarizes the whole syndrome.

We are well aware of the limitations of the United Nations. We are aware of the limitations of international legitimacy in its unfolding form. But at least the orientation should be to strengthen this international legitimacy rather than to show that it is totally meaningless. At the same time, there is the issue that Ms. Dayan raises, namely, that the Labour Party won by a small majority. Palestinian concerns are very concrete; they are not theoretical. They are not frameworks; they are not general things. I can tell you one thing: since [the International Peace Conference on the Middle East at] Madrid, the amount of day-to-day pressure on the Palestinian population has increased by leaps and bounds. I am not speaking about deportations, and I am not speaking about detention or death squads or undercover units. I am speaking about small things that add up to too much. For someone from Ramallah, it is a big deal to come to pray in East Jerusalem. For someone from Gaza to come and study at my university, it is a big deal. For someone to get permission to go out, for someone to license a car, at every level it is a big deal. When we see the phenomenon of stabbing, the question that should be put is: What is it that places a man or a woman in a situation where he or she takes a kitchen knife and goes into the street, and regardless of who the victim is—whether a 13-year-old girl or a boy working in a school, and without knowing these people at all—simply stabs? It could be a soldier or a guard, or it could often be a Palestinian. We have increasing crime. What is it that creates such a sick cycle? It is desperation and it should be seen in this respect. You see someone do such a thing, and you know that people who perpetrate these acts are probably not going to survive them. They are not going to get a medal for them. They are not going to get cheered for them. Many of these acts are totally senseless and this is not a question of loving peace or what have you. It is simply something which most of the time is not even a result of organized activity. It is just people breaking up. If you put pressure on one and a half million people in their every movement, in every little thing, and you are constantly after them, someone, somewhere, somehow, is going to crack, and this is the kind of situation we are facing.

Then when someone says *Allahu akbar*, "God is great", it is immediately associated with this bogey of demonizing Islam. That is unfortunately becoming the rule of the day and all kinds of elements are playing into this demonization.

It is extremely important to note that what the Palestinians are looking for is concrete results. They are not looking for frameworks. They are not looking for nice set-ups here where we could appear to be getting along together. In fact, we know that behind this appearance of togetherness, we have people down there who are suffering brutally. And that is what has to be stopped. When we speak about fundamentalism, I do not want to go into the "us and you" kind of arguments. I am much more concerned in my daily life, living in the Old City of Jerusalem, with Israeli fundamentalism. I am not trying to reverse things. But concretely, the people who are threatening my neighbourhood on a day-to-day basis are, unfortunately, Jewish fundamentalists, with one difference: the world is not mobilizing and ringing the alarm bells. They are people who have tremendous financial support, not only from fanatics but also from Christian Zionists, especially in the Protestant world, who see everything that happens in the neighbourhood as a result of the revelation of the will of God.

In addition to this, there is a whole process of building on negative terms, seeing Islam, for example—a world of 1.2 billion inhabitants—as being outside the norms of universal values. This is something that can evoke only the worst feelings in people. Once you demonize people, in a way you also convert them to demons, and this is the kind of vicious circle we are facing.

Thus it is very important to understand the attitude of those who say that the United Nations does not count, that the United States does not count, that it is only Israel that will decide, and when it decides, it will be only out of sheer self-interest. For me, as a Palestinian, this attitude is a very advanced form of terrorism.

MODERATOR

Before we go further into the discussion, I should like to comment on observations made by Ms. Dayan regarding the United Nations. As a representative of the United Nations, I cannot let such remarks go unanswered. The United Nations today, after the cold war, is no longer a sideshow. The international community has accepted that United Nations resolutions, particularly the resolutions of the Security Council, are binding on all Member States, not only Member States directly concerned by these resolutions, but the States comprising the entire membership of the United Nations.

Today the United Nations is present in many regions of the world for peace-keeping, peace-building and, in some cases, peace enforcement. Therefore, in the interests of everyone, I think we should look at the United Nations a little bit more seriously, and stop considering it as something not worthy of the respect of public opinion or the respect of Member States.

YAEL DAYAN

I have been misquoted twice here, in five minutes. I did not say the United Nations does not count. I did not say it should not be given support. I said very clearly, and I repeat it, that the United Nations unfortunately will not be the body to resolve even the terrible massacre and rape and massive genocide that are happening next door to you in Yugoslavia. It will be supportive, it will certainly be instrumental, but it will not be the body that will give the Palestinians a Palestine. I made it very clear when I said that that is in Israeli hands, and I was very honest in saying to you that, in order for it really to happen the way we both want it to happen, it will have to be an Israeli majority decision.

And I do not think I deserve—for being not only honest but totally realistic about these matters and putting them in a positive light, for saying that we have a Government now, finally, that wants and is able to achieve peace—I do not think I deserve, for this, to be called the worst kind of terrorist.

PERICLES PAGALOS *(Amnesty International)*

I have two questions, one for Ms. Dayan and the other for Dr. Musallam.

First, for Ms. Dayan: Israel has been accused in the past year, and quite recently, of a continual breach of human rights, the violation of human rights, in the occupied territories. Don't you think that enforcing the human rights concept would be a step forward in negotiations?

For Dr. Musallam: Does the PLO accept the full range of human rights protection?

YAEL DAYAN

I have been fighting for human rights for many years, first from the outside and now in Parliament. There is no question that Israel is violating human rights. There is no question that this cannot be tolerated. There is no question that we do not see a way to impose a real solution from the outside. It was tried. Now, finally, we are close to the only solution that is possible, and that is the end of occupation, and so the entire question of human rights will no longer be in the hands of the occupier. This issue is not a question of degree. From my point of view, it is not even abstract. There is no such thing as a "good occupation", even if human rights were less violated and if they were more respected. Occupation would still be the worst evil there is and the worst deprivation of all basic rights, human, civil, political—call them whatever you like.

I am not saying this as an excuse. I am not saying, let's continue violating until the occupation ends. We see now that the result of occupation is terrible, a total violation of human rights. I do not intend to enter into any kind of symmetry here, but I have got something to say also about terror, about lack of recognition of Israel, and about things that I would also expect international bodies to be aware of, such as racism and the killing of Jews because they are Jews. If we explain everything by saying, well, this is the result of the terrible occupation, then that goes for both sides. If terrorism is only the result of a terrible occupation, and the violation of human rights is also of course a side-effect, indeed the nature of occupation, then obviously we must do whatever we can to stop the occupation so both sides—and granted there is no symmetry—will be able to benefit.

SAMI MUSALLAM

Let me state the position of the Palestine Liberation Organization on human rights. First of all, immediately after the establishment of the PLO, we signed the Geneva Conventions [of 1949] and the agreements on the International Committee of the Red Cross, which govern the International Red Cross associations. We attend their meetings and we find ourselves obligated and bound by the International Covenants on Human Rights.

We do this not simply because we have a self-interest in defending our people under the occupation *vis-à-vis* the constant violation of their human rights, but also because we think that human beings have their own values, moral as well as material, which have to be recognized, defended and protected. So we do recognize all these covenants on human rights. We have our own human rights organizations and we have our legal system as well. You can ask the Red Cross about our legal system. I have written a booklet, a long article, on the PLO infrastructure in which this is also tackled. So we do recognize all these issues.

I now want to comment on a very important statement concerning fundamentalism made by Ms. Dayan. I was struck by the symmetry which she in fact expressed about PLO terrorism, and her claim that occupation is the worst kind of breach of human rights.

First of all, we do not commit any acts of terrorism. What we do or what our people do is resist occupation, and Ms. Dayan has recognized that there is no such thing as a "good occupation" or a "bad occupation". All occupations are bad and the best way to stop all excesses is to end the occupation, and thus all human rights will be saved and protected and all human lives would also be saved and protected. The best thing for us in Palestine, and for those in Israel, is to see very quickly an end to the occupation, which for them would mean peace and stability and for us would also mean peace and stability where we can both develop our infrastructures in the manner which our peoples deem necessary and fruitful. That would be one way of solving the fundamentalist issue.

SARI NUSSEIBEH

I have a comment to make which maybe you will find rather surprising. I want to side here with Yael Dayan against my colleague Albert Aghazarian. In relation to the question of whether or not what she was saying can be in fact counted as a form of terrorism, I am sure that he did not truly mean it in that way.

What I want to say is the following. I think what I understood Ms. Dayan as saying, and it is certainly something I share with her myself, is that, in the final analysis and beyond the United Nations and the United States and everybody else whose role is definitely very important, it is Israel and the Israeli people who will have to give the kind of acceptance to the Palestinians that the Palestinians need in order to set up their own State and to live in their own homeland.

In the very same way, in fact in the final analysis, it is also the Palestinians and only the Palestinians who can give Israel and Israelis the kind of legitimacy and acceptance they need to live in the Middle East as a State. What Ms. Dayan is basically saying, what I understood her to be saying, is simply that you need to have the acceptance by the two peoples of each other in real terms in order for the two peoples to be able to live at peace next to each other. I think this is a point that has to be clarified.

EVANGELOS MAHERAS *(World Peace Council)*

The World Peace Council and all similar peace organizations support the decisions of the United Nations and of its Security Council on international matters and problems and therefore also on the Palestinian problem and conflict, and support the implementation of those decisions not only in specific cases such as the case of Iraq or now in Yugoslavia, but for all problems, Palestine, Cyprus, and so forth.

In October 1992 in Florence, there was an international meeting on the Palestinian question. It was continued in Malta in March 1993. In both meetings we had the participation of five peace organizations from Israel. The five of them declared that they accept the United Nations resolutions on the Palestinian matter as they are. Therefore they do not accept simply autonomy but also self-determination and the creation of an independent Palestinian State. They did not ask for any change in borders or negotiations on borders, and they also accept the United Nations proposal for Jerusalem. Only one of these five groups said that it might reconsider the point of Jerusalem.

These are my questions for Ms. Dayan: Are the positions of these peace organizations in Israel widely known in the country? Do they influence public opinion, and are they taken into consideration by the present Israeli Government?

YAEL DAYAN

I wish that the peace camp and these organizations, or others that accept all the good things the Security Council has decided, were a majority. Not only are they not a majority, but until recently they were quite marginal. They were even more marginal than their power in Parliament would indicate. In other words, a political party is usually less extreme or less definite in its views than a street movement or a protest movement. It is very easy to go on the barricades in the name of Peace Now or any protest movement holding out for the maximum. But when a political party really wants to be effective and reach a vote and have a number of hands that will change decisions, it has to compromise.

I do not know which five organizations were so supportive of all the Security Council decisions. The situation in the Israeli street, which will evolve as soon as people can see something with their own eyes, is one where you have more than 50 per cent of the population in favour of, in the wide sense of the word, territorial compromise, that is, peace for territory. This sentiment see-saws with relationship to the Knesset. Before, we had more than 50 per cent, but in the Knesset we did not have a majority. Now we have a majority, but the percentage has gone down as terror goes up, and it will go up when the talks produce the beginning of a good result. It will certainly reach 70 to 80 per cent if a solution is being offered that is acceptable to both sides.

Those organizations do not represent any kind of majority of the Israeli people on the question of Jerusalem. I think the last poll was something like 88 per cent in favour of Jerusalem's remaining united as it is the capital of the State of Israel. So there is still a very long way to go before people express themselves openly and say, yes, maybe there could be some compromise on Jerusalem. I think that this is premature now.

But generally, on stopping the occupation, on getting out of the territories after a successful interim period, I think that we can reach 70 per cent once the process begins and violence is reduced.

MOSHE AMIRAV

With reference to the last question, which relates to opinion in Israel *vis-à-vis* United Nations resolutions, I should like to mention the fact that around this table and among Israelis and Palestinians there is one consensus. We are united in rejecting United Nations [General Assembly] resolution 181 (II), which has to do with Jerusalem, and with the very fact that two parties are claiming Jerusalem for themselves. We are definitely united in the sense that neither wants Jerusalem to be internationalized, as proposed in resolution 181 (II).

Another point I should like to raise concerns the type of conflict we are dealing with. It is not the type of conflict you people here in Greece have with Turkey or any other country, in the sense that this is basically a psychological conflict that has to do with legitimization.

There were times in which the Palestinians did not give legitimization to the Israelis. There are new times now in which many Israelis do not give legitimization to the Palestinians. When we come to the question of Jerusalem, this becomes highlighted and crystallized.

Now this is not a question of security, like the rest of the conflict. It is psychological. It involves understanding what kind of partnership we are going to have in this very small city. The answer could be that this is a process, as is every psychological development.

We had for years in Israel a readiness to give up territory. This is a process that went from 20 per cent at the end of the 1960s to something like 60 per cent today. We are speaking today about the readiness of Israeli public opinion to accept a Palestinian State. This

Aghazarianis something that even 10 or 15 years ago was favoured by about 5 per cent. The percentage has risen to 25 per cent, maybe 30 per cent, today.

Speaking about the Golan Heights, if you had asked Israelis 10 years ago about the Golan Heights, you would have found between 2 and 3 per cent ready to give them up. In the last surveys we have in Israel, about 20 per cent of Israelis are ready to give up the whole of the Golan Heights. You will find 40 per cent ready to give up part of them.

So in other words what I am speaking about is a process. In this process, Jerusalem is the most difficult issue. But even on Jerusalem this process works.

TASSOS KOSTOPOULOS *(Eleftherotypia)*

Regarding the retracing of borders mentioned by Ms. Dayan and the solutions that the present Government of Israel is considering: What will be left for the Palestinian homeland? Are there any areas of the West Bank that are considered non-negotiable? What is going to happen with the settlements? Are some of them going to be given special consideration for strategic reasons?

I should also like to ask: How does Ms. Dayan evaluate the role of the Labour Party in the first period of the *intifadah*?

For Dr. Musallam, I have a question: What kind of retracing of the borders can be accepted by the PLO?

YAEL DAYAN

The present Government does not have a map. And if it had a map, we would not need 18 months, or one month or one week, for negotiations. The present Government talks, right now, about the interim period and not beyond. I hope the whole process will be accelerated. We talk about three years, and no later than three years, to begin discussing borders and the definitive status of the Palestinians. I think that if self-rule goes well, the whole thing can be made to go faster. There is nothing sacred about five years or three years or six months. If self-rule works and both sides are ready for it, I think they will have an interest in speeding it up.

As for the question of borders, as a starting-point each side wants the maximum. The Palestinians certainly demand to go back to the 1967 borders, and the Shamir Government would not speak about any repartition of the area. We are talking about borders that will give the larger number of Palestinians independence from Israeli sovereignty and will give Israel maximum security.

Security does not have to be measured only by permanent borders. When we talk security, we are also talking about some interim arrangements that will mean access. I shall give you, as an example, free sky for the Israel Air Force even over areas where we are not sovereign. This means that no other aeroplanes, no other fighter-bombers, can use the airspace. We had the same agreement with Egypt. It means also that no Arab army can cross the Jordan westwards.

This does not mean that our international border with the Palestinians will be on the River Jordan. Prime Minister Rabin calls it a security border for an interim period. What we are saying is that demilitarization includes prevention of any army from crossing the Jordan River towards the West Bank. I don't want to sound condescending and I definitely don't want to give advice to the Palestinians, but I think basically it is in their interest as well. We are talking about these kinds of borders. We are not talking about a map.

We have an argument inside the Labour Party. There is one Labour map that is ancient already and some people still believe in it. We are talking about annexation, additional annexation of borders in an area that was State land which is free of population and which would be, for security reasons, specifically to the north of the Dead Sea and in the southern part of the Jordan valley, south of where the border used to be.

I do not think this will work. I think State land which cannot be proven as an absolute security necessity will not enter into consideration. Altogether security today is not a question of where you hold the ground. It is a question of an arsenal on the one hand, and a deterrent force on the other. Security is also the kind of peace you achieve.

The big change in public opinion and inside the Labour Party is that security is not measured by the distance of the next Arab village from the border and not in the variety of hand-grenades. The components of security include economics. Peace itself is one of the components of security, and that is a big difference. Security will never be achieved unless there are peace and normalization. This is the state of mind and concept that the Labour Party is entertaining.

I would hesitate to go into maps. There are arguments. Everyone has got his idea of what is the one centimetre of the map that Israel cannot do without. I would leave it to the negotiations and I think there will be a good agreement when they come to that because there is no interest whatsoever in creating a Palestine which does not include 99 per cent of the Palestinians who are in the West

Bank and Gaza. It is a question of population. We are not going to squeeze them into an area that is smaller than what they had. The corrections will be minor.

Concerning settlements, yes, they are a problem because, as was said before, the Labour Party was part of the Government that encouraged certain settlements. There was a security reason for some of them but today we can be very definite about it, and there is a Supreme Court decision on it. Settlements are not a security asset to the Israel Army or to the State of Israel. Not only are they not a security asset, but they are a terrible burden. This was confirmed by the Supreme Court during the Shamir Government and there is no way that anybody, not even Mr. Rabin as a general or any of the Labour hawks, can claim that one settlement in the West Bank, and certainly not in Gaza, is in any way a security asset. One platoon of good soldiers or one guard station or one overflight, not even touching ground in the area, is more a security asset than six settlements or a city in the West Bank. They are a burden security-wise and budget-wise, and they certainly are a burden politically.

This does not mean that Israel is just going to take the lot and impose a transfer back to Israel on the settlements. They will have to face a variety of options and I expect we are going to have a lot of security problems with regard to their lack of enthusiasm to be dismantled. We are not going to impose dismantling on them. They will have the option of whether to live under Palestinian sovereignty or to come back home. The option they will not have is to claim the protection of Israel Defence Forces to stay where they are as Israeli citizens. Once the territories are no longer under Israeli sovereignty, the Israel Army is not going to be responsible for anything other than the security of the State of Israel within whatever its boundaries will be.

I have nothing good to say about [the] Labour [Party] during the first stage of the *intifadah*. I have nothing good to say about anybody's treatment of the *intifadah*. I don't know whether they had a choice. I am going to revert here to my basic premise that I can say almost anything, and if I am quoted in Israel, it will not be my downfall. I have been in this situation many times recently. I can almost say that I wish the *intifadah* had occurred earlier, because the lack of *intifadah* in its resistance form created an illusion in Israel, especially under the Unity Government, the Likud and the Labour Coalition Government, that something good can happen from the occupation, that the occupation is not so terrible, that Palestinians are accepting it, that they will get used to it, they will disappear, or a miracle will happen. There was no pressure for so many years to make the Government realize that the situation is never going to end until there is an actively sought solution. When the *intifadah* came, the Government saw nothing substantive in it, otherwise, so it believed, the uprising would have happened before. So the reaction was to overreact, and very badly at that, and I don't have one good word to say about the measures taken by [Prime Minister] Rabin—Mr. Rabin then or Mr. Rabin now. I have got a lot to say against the occupation. I have nothing to say against the *intifadah* other than it waited too long, but it certainly produced the results it should have produced.

SAMI MUSALLAM

I think the question of whether we will accept modifications of the boundaries or not has something to do with the negotiations. We believe, as I said earlier, that it depends on whether the Israeli side accepts the application of [Security Council] resolution 242 (1967) to these territories, which means the inadmissibility of acquisition of territory by force, and which means also the withdrawal from all the occupied territories including Jerusalem. There is a tendency in Israel, or at least as we see it, to distinguish between giving us self-rule and keeping sovereignty on the ground. This does not work with us.

What we have suggested for the negotiations is the Palestinian Interim Self-Government Authority (PISGA). During the negotiations all these issues should be discussed, including the transfer of power from the Israeli occupation authority to the Palestinian authority that will result from the negotiations.

We do not accept the difference between security settlements and political settlements. After all, both are settlements and we are talking of an area, the West Bank, which is a bit more than 5,000 square kilometres, of which Israel has already confiscated one third in order to enlarge the municipality of Jerusalem. So there is not much room for territorial compromise if one third has already been confiscated, and we have to renegotiate the remainder in order to find a solution.

SOVEREIGNTY; CITY GOVERNMENT: CREATIVE SOLUTIONS

3

PANEL

Dr. Sari Nusseibeh   *Mr. Moshe Amirav*
Dr. Ruth Lapidoth   *Mr. Hanna Seniora*
Dr. Albert Aghazarian

SARI NUSSEIBEH

First of all, I should very quickly point out that although I am a member of the Steering Committee of the Palestinian Negotiating Team, it is not in that capacity that I shall be speaking, but as an individual. My comments are therefore simply those of an individual Palestinian setting forth some ideas.

I should like to refer, very briefly, to a remark that was made by Ambassador Keeley this morning regarding the history of Jerusalem and the fact that it is the city that has more than any other suffered from continued conquests. I was reminded of growing up as a schoolboy reading about the history of Islam and Jerusalem, and I was always surprised by the stories or the traditions we were made to learn about Islam coming into Jerusalem. We were, of course, taught about a lot of Islamic heroism and conquests and military feats and so on, victories that were undertaken by Muslim armies. But unlike all those stories, the story we were given to learn about Jerusalem is really very unique and stands uniquely in my memory. It is the story of how Islam came into Jerusalem peacefully. The tradition that is recounted is that of a caliph and his manservant coming by themselves, without an army, across the desert into Jerusalem. Regardless of the facts in the case, this is the tradition that we were made to learn—that they came into Jerusalem and took the city peacefully.

I think there are two very important points about this story that we were being taught. One concerns the relationship between Jerusalem and a human being. While other cities are cities that man can conquer militarily, Jerusalem is not such a city. The only way to enter Jerusalem is to enter it peacefully and the only way to be part of Jerusalem is to do so peacefully.

The other aspect of the story which is, I think, also very important is that of the caliph and his manservant coming with only one camel, and they would exchange positions when one or the other would get tired. So the caliph would get off the camel and let his manservant ride, and thus they would proceed, alternating, until they got to Jerusalem. The symbolism here has to do with the equality of men before Jerusalem. I thought I would mention this because it is something that is very important in the Islamic tradition of how we see Jerusalem.

Let me now come to the subject at hand—sovereignty. The problem of contested sovereignty is complex but not inscrutable. The approach to a firm and therefore sustainable solution must be guided by the principle of parity, or balanced equilibrium. What Israel desires or claims for itself, it must also recognize for Palestinians. Especially in Jerusalem, an obvious lack of parity, an excessive possessiveness or exclusivity, is a certain recipe for disaster.

It is in God's city that the Arab-Israeli, Palestinian-Israeli, Muslim-Jewish war will be settled in peace once and for all or where the Arab-Israeli negotiations will crumble and totally collapse.

Now, one way of sharing the city and dividing sovereignty is simply and directly by the drawing up or the redrawing of physical, tangible borders. One ready-made principle for delineating such a border is the territory-for-peace-exchange principle embedded in Security Council resolution 242 (1967), on which the present peace process is predicated.

Israel's acceptance of its formal withdrawal to the 1967 lines would automatically render all acts unilaterally taken by it since June 1967 as null and void, as indeed they are, *de jure*. Proceeding from this basis, negotiations can take place on the status of Israeli citizens and properties that will be left in Palestinian sovereign territory as well as on the modalities or the nature of the border itself.

Such negotiations on status, as well as on modalities or nature, can generally be guided by the same principle which will guide the negotiations over the cross-country or inter-State border that will divide the Israeli and Palestinian States. But because of Jerusalem's religious and historical distinctness, special provisions can probably be made to allow for freer cross-border fluidity in the movement of people, goods and services, as well as for extraterritorial administrative authority or authorities over religious sites.

The benefits such a solution will have are obvious. Furthermore, the model need not be regarded as a closed-system model, but as one that allows for the integration of various additional modular structures, for example, relating to various forms of cross-border functional cooperation at the municipal or the governmental level.

The disadvantages for Israel are also obvious, since Israel will have here to renounce or go back on its claim to exclusive sovereignty over Jerusalem and it will have to accept a border limitation to its free-handed policy in the city. However, this is a cost, in general, that Israel will have to sustain in one form or another if the principle of parity is to be upheld.

Perhaps slight border adjustments can be incorporated into this model to account for various requirements, for example, religious or cease-fire anomalies. But the main principle will be the existence of a tangible, continuous borderline, clearly marking separate, distinct sovereignties on either side.

Now another way of distributing rights of sovereignty is by sharing rather than by separating, where shares are not of specific locations but of the aggregate whole, rather analogously to the way the whole country might be shared by the two peoples in the context of a single binational State rather than be physically sliced into two sovereignties for two States, or to the way two States might share a trans-border aquifer, or two riparian States might share rights to a river or a lake.

By necessity, if this principle were to apply to Jerusalem it would require having Jerusalem turned into a *corpus separatum* with a status distinct from that of the two sharing States. But its status as a *corpus separatum* in this context would be different from that designated or defined for it by the United Nations partition plan, which was referred to this morning. Obviously it would have to have a separate legal status because of the way in which the sovereignty of the two nations is to be defined.

However, and in view of the paper that you have in front of you, the Amirav boundary and demographic expansion proposal,[1] a proper application of this principle would require the distribution of equal rights, regardless of population figures, since the distribution would be among the nations or national sovereignties sharing the city rather than among the population itself or its residents. In other words, demographic disequilibrium or imbalance should not be prejudicial in favour of the numerically dominant population. In any case, if we take into account the context in which demographic expansion has taken place over the past 25 years, we realize that this is an unfair basis, and rights should be represented not in accordance with the number of stock owners but in accordance with the number of stocks themselves. The point here is to distinguish between whether, as you share sovereignty, you do it among the nations as national groups and therefore with parity between the two nations, or among the individuals, therefore making the demographic situation more important. I don't think it should be regarded as important.

A salient feature of such a model, in contrast with the first model, is the absence altogether of any boundary or borderline

---

[1] See annex III.

within the city itself. The two States can jointly run the city and its functions through their representatives and in accordance with the body of agreements reached between them on the issue, regulating both intra-city as well as trans-city affairs.

Again the benefits of the model are obvious and the model itself can serve as the baseline for incorporating additional modules as and when needed. Certain adjustments, for example, to the metropolis boundaries can also presumably be countenanced at no risk to the model itself.

But the disadvantages from the Israeli point of view are also very obvious. The difference for both sides would be, but more for the Israeli side perhaps, that in the first model, a relatively free hand is countenanced for activity on one side of the border solely because Israel will only be able to conduct its activity on its side of the border, whereas in the second model, on the other hand, the expansion of rights of activity across that border can be achieved only at the cost of reduced rights on the first side. So for each there is a price to pay.

However, what this model provides for, which the first one does not, is sovereign access to or sovereign rights in at least those parts of the other side that may be held essential for one reason or another, for example, properties, people or religious sites. In the first model, of course, these sites or people might be located outside of sovereign boundaries or borders, and their status would have to be negotiated accordingly.

Another advantage of this model is that complete binational cooperation and sharing of municipal functions at all levels would be an essential ingredient of the baseline system rather than a limited set-up which is a separate, though an additional, module, as the case would be in the first model.

Now, in their extreme versions these two models lie on opposite sides of the spectrum. However, it is possible to countenance modular additions to either model in the direction of making the one approach or grow into the other. With some limitations, however, in both models the basic premise or principle that was used is the premise of parity of sovereign rights. Sovereign parity was defined in two ways, that of separating or splicing on the one hand or that of integrating or sharing on the other. In terms of theoretical simplicity, the first model is more attractive. In terms of aesthetic and perhaps even moral value, the second model is more attractive.

In real life, of course, Israel wishes to maintain the unity of the city without having to yield on dividing or sharing sovereign rights at all. And this is actually not only going to be useless, not only going to be unacceptable and not only going to be or is actually offensive, but it is also an extremely dangerous recipe.

Now finally, and against the background of the two versions I mentioned, I should like also to add here that it is obviously quite possible to construct a third model which is a mixed version of the two I explained. A basic sovereign line may be kept which is porous (or permeable) and invisible enough on the one hand to allow for a maximization of sharing, but which is substantive enough on the other hand to allow for the required degree of separation. It may be continuous enough to maintain an adherence to the historic "green line", but discrete or disjunctive enough to allow for the existence of disjoined or scattered sites of sovereignty. In this way, parity of sovereign rights can be maintained as a basic principle, but the correct mixture of dividing and sharing, separating and integrating, will optimize the benefits accruing to the two communities from the implementation of these rights.

My remarks have obviously been very telescopic and shallow, but I hope that there are some ideas in them that are worth exploring.

In conclusion, I should like to make a quick comment on procedural issues and again refer back to one of Ambassador Keeley's remarks this morning with which I totally agree. Deferring the issue of Jerusalem might make it easier to begin a process but it certainly would make it highly questionable that we could end this process successfully. In contrast, choosing to tackle the issue directly and head-on might be more difficult to begin a process, but if the process has begun on this basis, it is certainly far easier to imagine that one can ensure a successful end. And it is in this spirit, I think, that the Jerusalem issue should be addressed as quickly as possible in the negotiations.

MODERATOR

Thank you, Dr. Nusseibeh, for your most imaginative remarks. I hope that the audience has seized on these remarks and that they will provide the occasion for an exchange of views that will be beneficial to all those involved in the debate on the issue of Jerusalem.

I now give the floor to Dr. Ruth Lapidoth, who is a professor of international law at the Hebrew University of Jerusalem. Dr. Lapidoth is certainly most qualified to address the issue of sovereignty, which is of course a legal issue according to international law.

RUTH LAPIDOTH

I have to tell you that I do not represent anybody in the country. I am not a member of any political party so I can say nasty things about all of them. Perhaps I represent my husband, but I am not even sure about that.

Usually when I lecture about Jerusalem, I have to explain both attitudes, but in this group I do not have to represent any specific attitude. I can just give my own opinion. But since I am a teacher, I must of course correct a few errors that were made this morning.

With regard to the demographic issue, I have to mention two facts. First of all, I have heard that since the unification of Jerusalem the Arab population of the city has doubled. Secondly, since the year 1830, which means under the Ottoman Empire, there has been a Jewish majority in Jerusalem.

Another matter which, Mr. Tlili, I should like to mention, is that you said that Security Council resolutions are all binding, but I think my students would say that some of them are binding, and most of them are recommendations. They are binding only if they are adopted under Chapter VII [of the Charter of the United Nations].

The first question that arises is: What about [General Assembly] resolution 181 (II)—can it serve as a basis for a solution? I do not think that it can be a solution for Jerusalem because it proposes internationalization. Not only is it that the two parties mainly involved, which means the Palestinians and Israelis, do not want internationalization, but history has told us that internationalization has not been successful in the past, and actually today no international territory exists. We should not get into trouble that is not absolutely necessary.

I would suggest that when we deal with the problem of Jerusalem, we should try to divide it up into its various components. Jerusalem has three main questions. One is the national question, the second is municipal arrangements and the third, arrangements for the Holy Places. I think that if we divide the problem into its three components, it might be easier to deal with.

There is the question, of course, of what the basis is of Israel's claim to sovereignty over the whole of Jerusalem. I leave that to the questions and answers, but don't forget to ask that question.

Concerning sovereignty, we have heard a very interesting analysis and discussion by Dr. Nusseibeh, and my proposals are not very different from his. The term "sovereignty" has a tremendously strong emotional appeal. People hate to make compromises on sovereignty because they feel that they are giving up something of themselves. On the other hand, the term sovereignty and the notion of sovereignty have lost a lot of their relevance in international relations in general.

If we hope to find a solution for Jerusalem, it is better that we should not dwell too much on the issue of sovereignty. People do not want to make compromises on sovereignty. But if we leave it aside, and if we say, "We divide functions, we give *functional sovereignty*" (and this term "functional sovereignty" does exist nowadays, for instance, in the law of the sea—and the Greek people know a lot about the law of sea, what with their problems about territorial sea and the exclusive economic zone, as well as the continental shelf, and they know that, with regard to some of these areas, there exist sovereign rights for the purpose of exploration and exploitation of natural resources, which means it is a matter of "functional sovereignty"), I do not see why we should not use a similar idea when we deal with Jerusalem because I am looking for a means to get people to agree on some kind of compromise.

Sovereignty can be suspended. It can be frozen. You know that in Antarctica, sovereignty has been frozen since 1959 in order to prevent clashes. Sovereignty can be functional. It can be differential. I think the easiest way to deal with sovereignty would be, simply, either to suspend it or to split it up into functional sovereignty for the purpose of various functions. Of course there has to be—as Ambassador Keeley said in the morning, and everyone agrees on that—freedom of access for everybody between the two parts of Jerusalem.

As to the boundaries, I think we can also have functional boundaries. One boundary would be applicable for strategic matters, another for commercial matters and a third for population purposes. It does not have to be the same boundary for every purpose, and with your permission I should like to read to you a passage about sovereignty which I found so interesting in an article published in *The Washington Post* in 1990. It is by [former United States Secretary of State] Mr. George Shultz, currently with the Hoover Institution:

"Today the meaning of borders is changing and so is the notion of sovereignty. In the Middle East, a vision is needed that transcends the boundaries of traditional nation-States and addresses the clear requirements for the part of security, political voice, economic opportunity and community life on an equal basis. Constructs based on absolute sovereignty and rigid borders cannot provide this vision. Thinking must increasingly be on a regional-wide scale. A little creativity about new mixes of sovereignty might help move the peace process forward right now.

"The juxtaposition of territory for peace need not be a matter of where to draw lines but how to divide responsibilities."

Before I finish, I want to tell you two stories, personal stories, because I think they are encouraging.

A few years ago one of my students in the Arab-Israeli seminar told me, "But listen, on Jerusalem we absolutely cannot make any compromise." I said, "What do you mean by compromise?" She thought a little bit about it and then said, "Well, I must be free to visit every part of Jerusalem." This was a very encouraging story. When she says no compromise, it means "I need the right to go any- and everywhere."

There is another story, which is from these very days—the closing of the territories and the borders between Israel and the territories. In the house where I live in Jerusalem, some of the cleaning jobs are done by a very nice gentleman from an Arab village who lives not far from Jerusalem. When the closure was imposed and he could not come and do his job, the whole house decided that we would continue to pay his salary and when the closure is ended he would perhaps give us a few additional hours and help us out.

I thought that these two optimistic stories might help us to get into a more optimistic mood.

ALBERT AGHAZARIAN

I am here as a Jerusalemite, a real Jerusalemite. And speaking about real Jerusalemites, I think that the Mediterranean people, according to Robert Fox in his book entitled *The Inner Sea*, whether they are Greeks or Spaniards or Algerians or Lebanese or Israelis or Yugoslavs, have common features. Among their common characteristics, first of all they like to interfere in the work of others. When they sit in a restaurant they want to know everyone at every table. And the second element that binds us is that we are self-aggrandizing. We think, all of us around the Mediterranean basin, that we are more important than we really are. As a Jerusalemite I belong to that tradition.

You know I am supposed to be speaking about creative solutions—that is what the programme in front of me says—but as I listened to the sessions today, I thought I would read to you my statement on creative solutions in the last two minutes of my talk. I want first to tell you this. I think we have to imbue our discussions with a new spirit, because really we are speaking about very profound issues. I think this Encounter will miss an opportunity if we do not address certain crucial issues in order to move towards the future.

When we speak of history in this context, we are speaking of a quarry where we cut stones and we hit each other with these stones, because there is not one single history. For me as a Palestinian, the conflict essentially is one which transcends national and political boundaries in its true cultural essence. This is a conflict between the pluralistic and the monolithic.

This is not a question of religion—Jewish, Christian and Muslim. That is too simple. Because Jerusalem, the way I explain it, the way I see it every day, the way I enjoy walking with my friends almost on a daily basis within its walls, is at its heart the Old City. To simplify it for tourists, they say that the Old City of Jerusalem is composed of four quarters. In fact this is an oversimplification. Within every one of these quarters I could show you sub-quarters. Armenians, for Greek Orthodox dogma, are heretics. Copts are heretics. Assyrians are heretics. Muslims do not follow the true prophet. The Jews killed Jesus Christ. But nevertheless they all live together. These feelings do exist no matter how much we want to step into a new world. All the tribal biases are always there.

So when we speak, for example, of the Christian quarter, you would have an area which is Greek Orthodox, and an area which is Roman Catholic. You would have an area which is Coptic or Assyrian. If you speak of the Muslim quarter, you have an area of people who came from Afghanistan, from Morocco, from Kurdistan. We have even gypsy Muslims, and the Sunni Palestinian community is integrated into this landscape.

Speaking of the Jews, not only do you have Sephardim and Ashkenazim, but also you had a rift between what is known in Jewish tradition as the Perushim and the Zedukim. And the Perushim were prevailing until 1877. These are people who already in the second century before Christ had the conviction that Jews in power are corrupt so they should stay away from power in order to maintain their morality. They were against the establishment and they were against King Herod. These, Christians know as the Pharisees. They are still around. They are part of the landscape.

When some Israelis say it is the right of a Jew to live anywhere in the State of Israel or in Jerusalem, I can challenge the Minister of Religious Affairs in Israel, who wears a *kippah*, to live in Mea She'arim, which is the religious neighbourhood of Jerusalem. I can assure you that they will lynch him for being unorthodox.

This is something that I know 100 per cent. I live in the midst of all that. I can take you around, Yael Dayan, any time you are interested. For me the life of Jerusalem is in the living stones. You have many ways of viewing it. I do not mind that, for the Greek Orthodox, Byzantium is crucial. The fact that the Bible was written in Greek is absolutely important.

For the Copts, one of the biggest events in history is the Holy Family taking refuge in Egypt. For the Muslims, of course, you have

Al Aqsa and the Edict of Omar, which symbolize Islam's tolerance of Judaism and Christianity. Everyone has a piece. We are speaking of a fragmented mirror and everyone is holding a piece of that mirror. He or she can see the reflection of what they want.

I am a historian, although I am not here to speak about history. I am supposed to speak about the future. I shall in due time.

In my opinion, the history of Jerusalem in a living form starts in 1831. This is a turning-point. Forget about all the past, the Romans, Byzantines and so on. For me, history as a living mechanism starts at a given point, in 1831. At that time the entire city of Jerusalem had 9,000 inhabitants: 4,000 Muslims, 3,000 Christians and 2,000 Jews—and this is from Israeli sources, Professor Lapidoth. Also it is verified. They were all living within the walls, which used to be locked at sunset. In 1831 there was an Egyptian campaign which, for the first time in the history of the region, created transcontinental alliances. Egypt was allying with France, and in return you had Britain coming to the support of the Ottoman Empire in order to meet this challenge.

I do not want to elaborate too much, but by 1839 this defiance was crushed owing to massive British support for the Ottomans. The British then came to collect their dues, together with other European countries, so we start the period of the *Tanzimat*, which is the period of perestroika of the time. This is a period when in fact European countries start having protégés within the Ottoman Empire.

It was enough for any Jew to come from anywhere in the world and, after a period of six months, be granted the status of protégé of the British Empire with all the rights and privileges therein. That is when the demographic changes started.

Since 1967, we have had major transformations in Jerusalem that cannot be ignored. During the war of June 1967 a historic Moroccan quarter was demolished in order to create the big plaza in front of the Western Wall. As a result, 620 people were expelled without any compensation, and with only two hours' notice. There was even a woman who was buried alive in the rubble. The reason given was to provide proper access to the Western Wall.

In April 1968, Pinhas Sapir, who was then Minister of Finance, signed an edict confiscating 120 dunums in the Old City, that is, about 40 acres of land, for reasons of public utility. The area in question was the area of the Jewish quarter as it existed in 1948, according to Israeli Zionist sources. In fact, the Jews never owned more than 20 per cent of this property. This was the property of local Palestinian Muslim families. The High Court after seven years of deliberations decided that while these families own property and have the property titles, they cannot live there because from 1948 to 1967 the Jordanians deprived the Jews of access. The High Court decision was intended to insure that every quarter maintains its own flavour, its own characteristics.

As a Jerusalemite, I am in love with every part of the city, with every group that is associated with Jerusalem, whether or not I agree with their views. But I cannot understand how in 1980 there could be a new wave of extremist settlers breaking into the Muslim quarter and claiming that this was the historic Jewish quarter. With tremendous funding and important political support from the Israeli Right, they have taken 53 buildings so far in the Muslim quarter. These people do not deny that they are openly anti-Christian, anti-Muslim, and that they are against Yael Dayan or any other non-agreeing Zionist Israeli. They stand up on the roof and they say, "Yael Dayan is a traitor".

These people impose themselves as our neighbours in a forcible manner and this is supposed to be "peaceful coexistence", with wire grills being the most recent addition to the architecture of the Old City. In 1990 we had the take-over of the Hospice of St. John, which is Greek Orthodox property, and when the Greek Orthodox Patriarch wanted to protest this take-over, he was tear-gassed with all the rest of us. The issue is still supposed to be in court, and everyone knows that the settlers live there in this place which they now call Neot David. It was known as St. John's Hospice because it is exactly next to the Chapel of St. John the Baptist, which is one of two chapels that survived the vicious invasion of the Persians in the year 614. For 14 years, as many Greeks should know, Heraclius resisted, and struck back in 628.

There are many kinds of issues here. The basic element I cannot accept is absolute Israeli sovereignty over Jerusalem. Very clearly, on a day-to-day basis, this has been a marginalizing experience that will eventually eliminate everything which does not fit into the establishment, including much of the richness and the diversity within Jewish life.

I happened to be in Madrid. My biggest personal problem, if I may say so, was posed by members of the Neturei Karta, who are a religious Jewish group with fur hats who were saying, "We are part of the Palestinian delegation" and who tried to organize a press conference for me. I felt that if we accept these people as members of the Palestinian delegation, this will definitely not go over with the media. But these people identify themselves as Palestinians and they are the people who live there, so we are speaking about complex issues.

It is encouraging that sessions like this open up these questions. It is a good thing to start to share this city despite all the religious and national fervour. I think there is a way to compromise on Jerusalem, if we really want to, and if the Israeli body politic realizes that this is not a city that can be purely Jewish in an absolutist sense. This is a city which transcends its political components, Palestinian-Israeli, because we have many groups that for 1,500 years have been associated with the place, yet do not have any political attachment. What are the Copts doing there? The Abyssinians? The Greek Orthodox still feel dogmatically that it is a Byzantine city. The tradition is that when Sophronius handed the keys to Omar, he handed the keys of earthly Byzantium, but divine Byzantium is eternal. So for them it is an Orthodox city.

Everyone has his piece of the mirror. Let us keep the diversity.

Now if you want to have a solution, there are many ways, and Mr. Amirav's group, the Israel-Palestine Centre for Research and Information, and others have been working hard on this. It simply requires eliminating from the mind of the Israeli body politic the *idée fixe* that this is a purely Jewish city. This mind-set puts aside everything that is non-Jewish. It only looks for the Jewish, so when they engage in archaeology, they only look for Jewish archaeology. When they want to speak about the different peoples belonging here, they speak as if the history of the place starts with King David. King David's Temple is gone. We have King Solomon: King Solomon's Temple is gone. History stops. We move to 1911, the year of the first kibbutz, and to 1948, and this is the way history is seen. There is nothing wrong with this, but what worries me is that behind this approach you have a mighty State with tremendous determination and with all the means to uproot all the other groups that belong to the landscape.

I shall now come to my original topic concerning city government and creative solutions. First of all, people should recognize the mutual right of self-determination and decide to make a real contribution towards resolving the conflict. There are many questions. Can we go in the direction of a positive-sum approach? Could the betterment of the economic, cultural and quality-of-life concept prevail? We live in a world of economic consumption where people's profits conquer ideology. Could material benefit, economic prosperity and tourism sort of remould people's stiff ideological, historical positions?

Maybe we need to provide the inhabitants with a special Jerusalem passport in addition to their national passports, to give them what could be a separate kind of identity which might create a special bond that could ameliorate the general national feeling.

Of course, we have to recognize Jerusalem as a focal point for both peoples. It is extremely important that this city belong not just to both peoples, but also to many other groups as well. I have no problem with the Orthodox Church belonging there. With all the different groups, Russians and Moldavians, the latest addition in our supermarket is the Mormons. You know they have a nice campus, and I think they are as much a part of the landscape as anyone else. This is the specialty of Jerusalem. This is being a Palestinian, really in a cultural sense, the diversity which defies attempts to monolithize the city. You cannot simply keep looking into one fragment of the mirror.

I think, of course, that Jerusalem has to be maintained physically open. There are ways jointly to determine geographic boundaries and the key word here is *jointly*, because what we have had there until now, since 1967, has been unilateral enforcement, and it is not the Moshe Amiravs who are running the show, people who at least, even if they are municipal officials making plans, are thinking about what Albert [Aghazarian] or others, or Arabs, or Palestinians might think. The people who are "calling the shots" are people who simply deliberately, and ideologically, want to keep everyone else out. They say, "You don't belong, everyone out". They say, "You were just squatting over the years. Now we've come back, go wherever you belong . . ". This is the attitude on the ground, unfortunately.

It is encouraging, in spite of the bitterness, that maybe there is a new way of seeing that this cannot go on. Maybe both parties should state that the aim is a prosperous, dynamic and vibrant community in which both Israelis and Palestinians play a full part. Agreement is needed on many issues and I think that if there is a will, there is a way. We must discuss the boundaries, division of authority, how to handle the questions of immigration and guaranteed free access. In fact, under Rabin's Government there has been greater difficulty in guaranteeing access to the Holy Places. Recently, we had the Feast of the Holy Fire, and people from Ramallah, or from Bethlehem, could not make it to the Holy Sepulchre in order to participate, together with the "Hajjina" or pilgrims who came from Greece for this celebration. So they said to themselves, "People coming from Greece have the right to pray and we who live here have no right to pray". I think these issues should not be taken lightly because it is part of the folk traditions and the collective history and practices of the place.

There is the need to demilitarize. I for one believe adamantly as a Palestinian that there is no point in arming. There are other things to spend money on. There is a need for a body that can arbitrate these issues. I think you could easily have an arbitration committee that could be composed of Israelis, Palestinians and maybe three international arbitrators, judges or experts in international law, to organize a formal police force and to discuss how it will be funded. There is the question of official languages. Even though Arabic is supposed to be an official language, you hardly ever see Arabic on signs.

Palestinians get their tax papers in Jerusalem completely in Hebrew, and even after all these years, there are few of them who speak Hebrew.

So of the options, I think there is a possibility of establishing two municipalities, to have a joint planning commission, to ensure access to the Holy Places and, most important, to maintain unity in diversity.

MODERATOR

Thank you, Dr. Aghazarian, for the wealth of ideas you have presented. Before giving the floor to Mr. Moshe Amirav, I should like to respect his request that I identify him in the following way, "a former Likud activist who now represents the Shinui Party on the City Council of Jerusalem and heads the Council's Committee on East Jerusalem Affairs".

MOSHE AMIRAV

I should like to start with a personal story to try to convey an idea that I believe will help to ease the situation, and maybe even solve it. The way I see the problem of Jerusalem is that the city is so loved and so adored by so many people. The problem is that today actually two peoples would like to see Jerusalem as their own city. I myself was a soldier, a paratrooper in the Six Day War, fighting in Jerusalem. I was wounded there, and nowadays I am invited by the IDF [Israel Defence Forces], by the Army, to give lectures to the young soldiers about Jerusalem, about the Wall, about victory, about what is going on in Jerusalem. I should like to tell my friend Sari Nusseibeh that I always start my lecture in front of these young soldiers with a story about one of the many, many conquerors of Jerusalem. His name was Omar. I tell this story, though he was not a Jew and definitely not an Israeli. The Caliph Omar was one of the very few conquerors of Jerusalem who came with basically a lot of humility towards the city. I tell these young soldiers how he went into the city and he went to the Wailing Wall and he ordered his 30,000 troops to clean up the area out of respect for the Jews, and I tell them that he didn't enter the Holy Sepulchre because he was afraid that if he did, later on a mosque would be built on this Christian place. I start with this story because I think that this is what young soldiers have to understand. This humility when we deal with Jerusalem. This humility that we Israelis, and not only Israelis, sometimes lack when we deal with the issue of Jerusalem.

The problem in Jerusalem is a psychological one. How can we Palestinians and Israelis both feel that this is "our" city, rather than "my" city?

As part of the solution there is a paper in front of you which contains some of my ideas.[2] It is a blueprint for a solution. This is just one idea, but the idea is important in that it is a way to try to see things in a kind of confederal way—one city, not divided, that will accommodate the two communities, because basically we are speaking about Palestinians and Israelis rather than the whole of world Christianity, Islam and Judaism. The two States have to have some national satisfaction. One way of doing it is by enlarging the municipal border. Actually when you fly over Jerusalem today by helicopter, you look down and what you see is no longer the city of Jerusalem we all knew before 1967. It's a new Jerusalem. It's a big Jerusalem. It's one conglomerate metropolis that spreads from Bethlehem in the south to Ramallah in the north, from Ma'aleh Adumim—which is a township in itself but also a suburb of Jerusalem—in the west to Mevasseret in the east. The solution has to be based on a kind of parity that my colleagues here were speaking about.

I would rather speak about the not-too-distant future, because what I have just outlined is something that will not happen tomorrow, maybe not next year. But I hope it will happen eventually. What can be done today? What can be done tomorrow in Jerusalem in order to prepare the infrastructure for this idea, and in order to ease things through and towards a peaceful solution? I would say that the main issue has to deal with the psychological infrastructure, the way Israelis see the city. We also have to induce a change in the psychological attitude of Palestinians towards the city, and I shall explain what I mean by that.

The main problems that the Palestinians have in Jerusalem today, besides occupation, are twofold. The first one is economic, especially with building dwelling units for the population. There is a big shortage of housing units for the Palestinians. The other one is the lack of representation. The Palestinians are not represented. The fact that I as a member of the City Council [of Jerusalem] sometimes help Palestinians on certain issues does not constitute representation. They do not have any representation; in a democratic system, of course, that means you lack not only the political power, but also budgets and other things that you deserve.

There is a new chapter in the life of Jerusalem since the election of this new Government, because this new Rabin Government

---

[2] See annex III.

is not only more flexible on the general peace process, it is also more flexible on the municipal aspect of Jerusalem, and I shall elaborate on that.

First, there is now, from the Government's point of view, a new approach that is ready to accept investments from outside, including Palestinian money that was not kosher before—even PLO money in projects in Jerusalem. The Government will always have a shortage of money to build in the Arab sector in East Jerusalem, but what is new is the readiness to accept investments from abroad for East Jerusalem.

Another thing that has to do with the municipality which is quite new is that we in the municipality just finished planning big parts of the city. It is very late. We should have done it in 1968 or 1969. Now finally we did it. This was after a lot of pressure from people like me in the municipality who complained about it. The fact is that as we speak we are finishing plans that will enable thousands of housing units to be built in all of Jerusalem, especially in the north of Jerusalem, in the Arab part of the city. These two things create a new opportunity for the Palestinians if they are ready to move on it, if they are ready to take in their hands their own destiny in Jerusalem. They can of course say they are waiting for the overall solution, but they can also say, "Okay, we will test the Israelis. We are ready to go with that".

What can they do? They can create development in East Jerusalem, and they do not need permission from the municipality or from the Government authority to do it. We can initiate projects in the three areas that are needed today for Palestinians—tourism, industry and new neighbourhoods, not houses built scattered, one here, one there, the way it is done today, but whole new neighbourhoods of 3,000 or 4,000 units built at once. This can be done soon.

The other problem has to do with representation. The Palestinian attitude since 1967 has been to ignore the western municipality and actually boycott municipal political life. I think it is high time, especially after the *intifadah*, to change this attitude. I think that today, when a Palestinian-Israeli dialogue is going on anyway, we have to start a political dialogue in Jerusalem. We can start by the Palestinians electing their representatives in a democratic system. We have in West Jerusalem a system of local neighbourhoods that are electing their representatives. There is also an idea that Hanna Seniora and others raised of having a shadow municipality of their own. Fine, that is also a way.

There is something else that is happening right now. In November, we are going to have municipal elections, and a new government will be installed in this city. There is a good prospect that the Likud right wing might win the elections for the first time in Jerusalem. The consequences of this will be very bad for both the peace camp in Israel and the Palestinians in Jerusalem. The Palestinians can and should be part of the process to prevent this situation by supporting the peace camp. They have two parties, Meretz and Labour, to choose from. They have the right to vote. They can do it. Another way would be to go with a party of their own—a municipal party, an Arab, Palestinian party—that would be, and I hope you are listening to what I say, the biggest party in the municipality. The Palestinian vote, about 60,000 to 70,000 votes, can create the biggest political party in Jerusalem. This is a new phenomenon, a breakthrough that would have a psychological impact not only on the Israeli population, but worldwide. I am speaking about things that can be done by the Palestinians with the help of the peace camp, things that are in the framework of the Israeli system, as a first stage if we want things to be changed. We want to make sure that options that are open now will not be closed in the future. These are very practical things that have to be done both on the Israeli side, in terms of the psychology of Israelis and having to do with elements of confederal solutions, and on the Palestinian side, which needs to adopt new attitudes towards political solutions in Jerusalem.

HANNA SENIORA

As the last speaker of the day, I should like to have the privilege of commenting not only on what has taken place at this session but also of using a little bit of my time to comment on what took place this morning. And I would start with His Excellency the Minister for Foreign Affairs of Greece, who presented a very cordial, optimistic view of the bilateral talks that are taking place today. But he also avoided discussing the issue of Jerusalem, and we do not know very clearly the position of the Greek Government on this. He stressed the religious aspect on a sort of partisan basis, and he talked about the Greek Orthodox Church and the importance of the Church to the Greek people and to Christianity. Here it is good to understand that even in this small dimension, there is something bigger than any unilateral action by one of the parties to the conflict, either the Israelis or the Palestinians. Jerusalem does not only pertain to Israel and Palestine. It has a bigger dimension which is that of Islam, Christianity and Judaism.

Mr. Tlili presented the legal, international situation, what we call international legitimacy, and the position of the United Nations on the subject. He said very clearly that there are resolutions of both the General Assembly and the Security Council, and that these resolutions stand. They have not been rescinded, and the living example of that is that in Jerusalem even the United States does not have an embassy. The only country that I know of that has an embassy in Jerusalem is a small Latin American country, Costa Rica, and even Costa Rica is having second thoughts about having its embassy in Jerusalem.

I should like to clarify one point that was mentioned by Ambassador Keeley, Dr. Musallam and others about deferring the issue of Jerusalem to the second stage of negotiations. Here there was even some scepticism as to whether we are ever going to have a second stage where Jerusalem will be put on the agenda.

The Palestinians proceeding to the Madrid Conference had assurances from the American side that East Jerusalem, according to Security Council resolution 242 (1967), is occupied territory exactly like Gaza, Hebron, Ramallah and Bethlehem. When we Palestinians talk about deferring the issue of Jerusalem to the second stage of the negotiations, we make a big distinction which I want especially the press here to understand. It is not the issue of East Jerusalem that we agreed to defer to the second stage of the negotiations. It is the issue of all Jerusalem, east and west. Today in the present negotiations, even in the interim stage, the transitional period, East Jerusalem, for us, falls under Security Council resolution 242 (1967) and therefore rightfully comes under the current bilateral negotiations on the arrangements between Israel and the Palestinians.

I want to comment now on some of the issues that our good friend and colleague in the Israeli peace camp, Yael Dayan, has raised. We feel that she tried to overemphasize the differences that existed between the previous Government, the Likud Government, and the present Rabin Administration. We as Palestinians understand those differences. But we want to emphasize, especially in the context of those who are looking from outside the problem, that on two main issues that are very concrete to the Palestinian people, there are very few differences between the Labour Party and the Likud. One of these issues is the right of self-determination of the Palestinian people. Neither the Labour Party nor the Labour Government, nor the previous Likud Government, recognized that right. On the fate of Jerusalem, Ms. Dayan clearly stated that the present Labour Government remains committed to the firm belief that all of Jerusalem, east and west, is the united capital of the State of Israel. So we should not delude ourselves about the supposed great differences on many issues between the previous Israeli Government and the present Government. On the main subjects that are fateful for both peoples, issues of peace and war in the region, there are still big gaps between the Palestinian and Israeli positions.

I come now to another topic: Islam. The media should not be deluded into targeting Islam as the enemy. Extremist religious groups are not an Islamic or Christian or Jewish issue. It has to be understood that the three faiths have many things in common. The three faiths are trying to create tolerance, good will and peace, but there are radical extremist religious groups in various sectors of all the populations of the region and throughout the world. There is, for example, Gush Emunim on the Israeli side.

And then there is the issue of resistance. Not all forms of resistance should be dehumanized by calling them terrorism. The late father of Dr. Sari Nusseibeh was among the first Palestinians more than 20 years ago who condemned terrorism or violent acts against unarmed civilians. But there has to be a differentiation between the legitimate right of the people to resist occupation and the dehumanizing label of calling it all terrorism. I remember very clearly that during the British Mandate, Jewish and Arab resistance was called terrorism by the British. Yet two terrorists of the past, the late [Menachem] Begin and Mr. [Yitzhak] Shamir, became Prime Ministers of the State of Israel.

I join Ms. Dayan in noting that there is a significant absence of official representation from Israel and the United States in this forum. Although we heard also that there is an unofficial blessing from the Foreign Ministry of Israel, it is nevertheless significant that those two parties are missing from this important forum's deliberations, which are spotlighting the future of Jerusalem. I believe that the presence of one of the co-sponsors of the Madrid process, the Russian Federation, is a significant element in finding a compromise solution to the conflict between Arabs and Israelis and between Palestinians and Israelis. I believe in a compromise on Jerusalem, something like what we have heard from the various speakers today, including Dr. Nusseibeh, Dr. Lapidoth and Mr. Amirav.

Earlier we heard the comments of an expert from the Foreign Ministry of Greece, my colleague Mr. Galanopoulos, who stated that Greece never recognized the occupied territories. He also noted that security does not come with land. He mentioned the example of Greece and Bulgaria in the north of Greece where the area separating both sides is less than 20 kilometres, and he compared it very specifically with Netanya and Tulkarm and the 15 miles separating those two towns in Israel and Palestine. I affirm that peace and security can come only through establishing stability and understanding and parity and equality flowing from recognition of the right of self-determination for both peoples.

I find Dr. Nusseibeh's elaboration of three options on the issue of sovereignty very challenging. The writing that I did on Jerusalem is very close to his third option, where the issue of Jerusalem will be defined by specific areas of Palestinian sovereignty and specific areas of Israeli sovereignty, and at the same time areas where disputed sovereignty can be resolved by sharing (dual) sovereignty.

Regarding these disputed areas, I believe that what is important in our discussions is that we are creating a process by which we can educate maybe first and foremost our two publics, the Israeli and Palestinian publics, as well as the Arab public, which is near us, and the Mediterranean and the international public. Through such meetings under the auspices of the United Nations and the Government of Greece, we can, if we are willing to find a peaceful, negotiated settlement between the two peoples, find a way through even complex issues like the future of Jerusalem.

I listened with great interest to the views of a very esteemed international expert, my colleague Professor Lapidoth, and I believe that, yes, we have to divide the issue of Jerusalem into three aspects, the national issue, the municipal issue and the religious issue (although here she classified it under Holy Places). But I differ in one respect: Why try to evade the issue of sovereignty by dividing it under the aspect and the term of "functional sovereignty"? I believe that maybe one way, and she mentioned it, is that both countries should perhaps discuss suspending sovereignty and let Jerusalem be run like Washington in the District of Columbia in the United States. Maybe we have to create the District of Jerusalem and the city would be called Jerusalem, D.J.

There are many Palestinians and Israelis involved in discussions on the issue of Jerusalem almost on a monthly basis. From such forums we can create ideas to educate our publics and present papers that can be discussed in the bilateral talks between the two nations.

I totally enjoyed and identified with both Dr. Aghazarian's and Mr. Amirav's presentations, especially Dr. Aghazarian's attempt to spell out to you the mosaic and richness of Jerusalem. This richness can be reinforced if we bring peace and understanding between the two peoples that reside in Jerusalem. He gave you the human dimension, which is very important to understanding the complexity of the issues over Jerusalem.

As to what Moshe Amirav talked about, it is true that both our peoples love and adore Jerusalem, and I think they are hugging it to death at the moment. While Jerusalem today in the eyes of the Israeli is a united city, it is actually divided by a wall of fear. There is no wall dividing East and West Jerusalem. Maybe there is the road that Mr. Amirav built, called Highway 1, which divides East and West

Jerusalem, but there is a wall of fear that Palestinians venturing into West Jerusalem and Israelis venturing into East Jerusalem deeply feel.

I believe that we have to discuss in the near future how to maintain the economic life of Jerusalem, because today that economic life, especially in East Jerusalem, has been strangled by the closure of the territories. Today East Jerusalem is like a ghost town. East Jerusalem lives and flourishes and is nourished by its surrounding towns of Bethlehem, Ramallah, Abu Dis, Bethany and A-Ram, and these towns and villages have been isolated from East Jerusalem because of the military closure.

While we recognize that the inclusion of Mr. Faisal Husseini in the delegation to the bilateral talks is a very important step, this is only a sort of a formalization of what existed before. But on the ground, Mr. Rabin has responded by continuing to create new "facts". He has drawn the borders of the Palestinian Interim Self-Government Authority (PISGA) and excluded East Jerusalem from any discussion or participation in the future, even if we reach that stage of a self-government arrangement.

I brought with me from Jerusalem a multi-coloured map of the city.[3] Down from the bottom is the south of Jerusalem, near the Bethlehem area. The upper side is towards Ramallah, which is the north of Jerusalem. The lighter pink area is West Jerusalem and you can see the old green line dividing East Jerusalem and West Jerusalem. The darker pink areas are the new "facts on the ground" that have been created by the Israelis since 1967. Almost 50,000 dunums have been expropriated from East Jerusalem and the West Bank to create new "facts". Before 1967 no Israeli lived in East Jerusalem. Today in 1992 we have 130,000 Israelis living in East Jerusalem and we have about 160,000 Palestinians living there. In the next two years when the 60,000 housing units that Israelis are building in East Jerusalem and the surroundings have been completed, we, the Palestinians in East Jerusalem, will become a minority in our part of the city. The yellow areas are the remaining ghettos of East Jerusalem surrounded by the pink areas and what is called green land. Green land represents the areas where Palestinians are forbidden to build. They are zoned as a green area theoretically for public use, but "public use" in the Israeli dictionary means that these areas will next be incorporated into the Israeli part of Jerusalem when Israel has digested what it has already taken. If you look at the southern part of the city, there is an area which is green with pink stripes. This is an area where Israel is trying to build another new neighbourhood. There is also

---

[3] See annex III.

in this green area farther to the west another place, near Walajah, where Israel is also trying to build another area, and in the northern part of the city near Shafad there is another part of the green area where Israel is building new "facts on the ground". So we should not forget the present in trying to discuss the future. Today the present Government, as did the former Government, is proceeding headlong in its plans to change the demography of Jerusalem with no challenge from the Americans or the international community.

FLOOR DISCUSSION

Dr. Idith Zertal

Mr. Sofianos Chrysostomidis

Ambassador Robert V. Keeley

Dr. Ruth Lapidoth

Mr. Wesley Johnson

Dr. Sari Nusseibeh

Mr. Theoharis Papamargaris

Mr. Moshe Amirav

Dr. Sami Musallam

Ms. Yael Dayan

Dr. Albert Aghazarian

Mr. Stefanos Vallianatos

IDITH ZERTAL

I am not from Jerusalem. I come from Tel Aviv, and therefore I don't know whether I have the right to barge into this holy community of Jerusalemites, but maybe I can bring a somewhat more secular contribution from the coastal plain of Israel.

When I ponder the difference between Tel Aviv and Jerusalem, I see more than a geographical distinction. Historians of culture discern a real polarity between both cities. If Jerusalem represents holiness and religion, Tel Aviv is the emblem of secularity. If Jerusalem has become the emblem of fanaticism and eternal convictions, Tel Aviv represents the pragmatic, classical zionism. The coastal plain as opposed to the rocky mountain of Jerusalem means also tolerance and pluralism as opposed to intolerance and exclusivism; relativism versus absolutism. The Tel Aviv perspective is therefore quite important. And the first remark I would like to make as a Tel Avivian is that everything relating to the conflict, from my point of view, is discussable, is debatable—even Jerusalem. We should secularize the problem of Jerusalem and make it a political one, not a religious or a theological one. This is a step that could lead us further towards reconciliation.

My second remark is that if you want another proof of the difference between the Shamir and the Rabin Governments, look at the question of the Jewish settlers that usurped quarters in the old, Arab part of the city. This was one of the crazy excesses of the later period of the Shamir Government. It is unheard of, and could not take place, under the Rabin Government.

My last remark concerns the story that my colleague, Professor Lapidoth, told us (and I hope she will excuse my remark) about the cleaning gentleman working in her house. To put it mildly, I did not like the story. I think it is an expression of the kind of colonial good will and generosity that is deeply rooted in people of good will in Israel. I am not talking about the people of bad will in Israel, but the people of good will like Professor Lapidoth. This is a kind of master-slave relationship that should be erased when the peace process arrives at a solution. I will be satisfied when Jews clean the houses of Arabs as Arabs are cleaning and doing the gardening in Jewish houses.

SOFIANOS CHRYSOSTOMIDIS *(Avghi)*

I should like to ask two questions. The first is addressed to Ambassador Keeley and the second to Professor Lapidoth.

(Ambassador Keeley is obviously the President of the Middle East Institute, but we here in Greece are used to addressing him as Ambassador.) During your commentary you said that it is problematic whether outsiders, as you call them, should or should not have a say in the final regulation of the Jerusalem question. My question is, do you think that an outsider, for instance the European Community, can play a positive role?

My second question, addressed to Professor Lapidoth, is related to what she said about how the insistence on sovereignty hinders compromise. The meaning of sovereignty could be changed in the case of Jerusalem or even in some cases suspended, she said. So my question to Professor Lapidoth is: If she were to go further in this line of thinking, how would she see a more general resolution of the Palestinian matter?

ROBERT V. KEELEY

Yes, I believe that there is a role for outsiders in encouraging the settlement of the Jerusalem problem, and that it should be addressed sooner rather than later. But they should not have a veto over the terms of the solution, which must be acceptable to all the inhabitants of the city. I think that the position of the United States Government has always been that whatever solution can be worked out by the parties would certainly be satisfactory to us, and I think we will maintain that position. So the role of outsiders is to be encouraging and not to rule out certain aspects of a solution, but rather to permit the parties to settle the problem between themselves.

RUTH LAPIDOTH

Allow me first to answer my friend Idith Zertal. I am very sorry that Jews do not clean houses in East Jerusalem, but this is not the question of a national dispute, this is a problem of the social or economic development of the various peoples. Now the children of the gentleman who cleans our house go to school and they will learn a profession. They will certainly not go on to clean houses, neither in Arab buildings nor in Jewish buildings, but this takes time.

Coming back to the question of sovereignty, let me say that I have tried to study the question during the past years, and very briefly this is what I found out. First of all, sovereignty in history has usually played a negative role, because sovereignty is a term which has been used in its true, absolute meaning and has therefore encouraged totalitarian regimes and expansionism. Nowadays, sovereignty is more limited, and everybody today agrees that sovereignty is subject to international law. But nevertheless the term still has a rather absolutist connotation. It is therefore difficult to make compromises when you deal with questions of sovereignty. Today sovereignty could perhaps best be defined as including three elements: the first is that the sovereign is fully subject to international law; secondly, he is not under the control of any other State; and thirdly, he is in fact able to exercise a fair amount of State power.

There have been recent changes in the whole concept of sovereignty because of various developments: first of all, the democratization of States; in the second place, there is the fact that there are many federal States, and in a federal State, by definition, sovereignty is more or less divided or shared; and lastly, States nowadays accept major international commitments and obligations which although in principle do not limit sovereignty in fact do. And you know, much better than I, the question of sovereignty as related to participation in the European Economic Community. Among other circumstances that have limited the notion of sovereignty is, for instance, the severe limitation on the right to use force under the Charter of the United Nations. Another is the fact that human rights have taken on an international aspect, and this is also a limitation on the sovereignty of the State. Practically speaking, I would add that borders are no longer under sovereign control owing to developments in the sphere of communications, and this makes it impossible to control the borders. Also, new modern arms go far beyond borders because they have such a huge range. In economics, when you have a change on the stock exchange in New York, the next minute it is known in Japan, and it has a lot of influence. So nowadays closed-border sovereignty does not in fact exist anymore. Therefore some thinkers or some philosophers, excuse me for using that term, have changed their idea about sovereignty and they speak about a loosening of monolithic sovereignty. Someone wrote, "sovereignty is a relative notion, variable in the cause of time, adaptable to new situations and exigencies".

Therefore, in recent writings and in recent claims of States you find expressions like dual sovereignty, divided sovereignty, *de jure* sovereignty and de facto sovereignty, and in Canada the Québecois have the notion of *souveraineté-association, souveraineté partagée*. I found in another book a distinction between negative and positive sovereignty, and, as I mentioned earlier, there is "functional sovereignty", which means sovereignty only for a specific purpose. We also have the philosophical idea of pluralistic sovereignty. So sovereignty has undergone many changes, and if we use the term in its old meaning, which is more or less absolute except for the fact that it is subject to international law, it will be very difficult to make compromises. Therefore, I thought that since sovereignty is more or less breaking up, it might be easier to find solutions if we leave sovereignty aside and try to find solutions that are not based on sovereignty and do not involve questions of sovereignty.

WESLEY JOHNSON *(Middle East International)*

I should like to address a question to Dr. Nusseibeh, and I apologize that this does not deal with Jerusalem, *per se*, but given the thought that we will eventually arrive at elections in the occupied territories and the formation of a ruling council, or administrative council, for the Palestinians, could you please explain the present thinking on what will happen to the military Government? I have read that there is some talk of forming permanent standing committees on a functional basis out of this apparatus. Will it eventually wither away or will it have some responsibility in the final settlement?

SARI NUSSEIBEH

This is a very interesting question. I do not have a ready answer for it. I do not really know exactly what is going to happen in the future with regard to the committees that you refer to, which have been proposed by Israel, by the way, not by the Palestinians. I do not know whether they will, in fact, be set up in the first place, because as far as the Palestinians' position is concerned, we propose that there be no mention of any such committee. On the other hand, there is obviously a need to set up some kind of coordination between the interim self-governing authority and Israel, but we have not actually gone to any specifics. We are waiting to work out the framework.

I am worried about what will happen in Jerusalem while talking takes place on the rest of the occupied territories. Will Israel continue to take upon itself unilaterally to set up new "facts"? If we are talking not only about East Jerusalem but about deferring the issue of the whole of Jerusalem, it seems to me that this is like talking metaphysics, which I can respect in a philosophical but not in a political context. In the mean time, even though the issue is being deferred, actually Israel is creating new "facts on the ground", whether in West Jerusalem or in East Jerusalem. So something has to be done. As we saw on Mr. Seniora's map, it will be very difficult to reach a solution and it is on Jerusalem that the whole peace process can either succeed or fall apart, and therefore we have to deal with the Jerusalem issue as quickly as possible.

THEOHARIS PAPAMARGARIS
(Greek Committee of International Solidarity)

Hearing the various presentations and the discussions so far, many things have been said about security, about the need for peace, and nobody doubts their importance. There is also a need for coexistence between the various religious communities within Jerusalem. But until now, my feeling is that we did not speak of any elements related to the social and economic factors in Israel and Palestine. Let me make a hypothetical point. Let's say that tomorrow peace is signed. What would happen with matters related to the Israeli settlements in the occupied territories? with the control of water resources? the control of the land of the former Palestine, the present Israel? Here is a different situation that arises from the dynamics of things over the past 45 years. We have a water consumption ratio per capita of 10 for Palestinians to 100 for Israelis. There is so much land for Israelis, so much less for Palestinians. Settlements can be found throughout this area. How will all these points be solved? I do not see any analysis or discussion of the daily reality, and this is surprising.

I should also like to hear comments on what we mean by a confederation. Can the problems of these 45 years not be solved in any way other than the creation of a confederation? So is this the only possible viable solution?

MOSHE AMIRAV

I think you are absolutely right in saying that both communities lack blueprints for specific areas. The Israelis have blueprints on how to conquer Damascus and Tehran but they do not have blueprints for every detail that has to do with taxation. What kind of relationship will there be between the Palestinian market and the Israeli market 10 years from now? These are issues that have question marks for both Palestinians and Israelis. On the other hand, I always say that reality is stronger than any idea, and there are things that are happening every day. In terms of the broader picture, I would say as an Israeli that I doubt if a Palestinian State as such can stand economically alone without Israel, disconnected from Israel. I would even say that I would prefer, from the economic point of view, confederative solutions that also involve Jordan, because we are such a small country both in terms of geography and economic might.

Speaking about Jerusalem, let me tell you very frankly that options are being closed every day even under the Rabin Government. On Jerusalem, there is an Israeli national consensus that includes the current Government, about creating "facts"—about building houses for Jews. We do not build for Arabs. We build for Jews. I mentioned the elections that will be held soon, in November 1993, which might close even other political options in Jerusalem. The answer should be given by both Israelis and Palestinians. Some of my questions that were referred to the Palestinians about the possibility of their initiative were not answered. So we should have a dialogue on, and in, Jerusalem. Both Israelis and Palestinians must act in order to avoid closing more options for the future.

SAMI MUSALLAM

Any viable social policy that can be made for Jerusalem from our perspective—I am not speaking from the Israelis' perspective because they are in control—means first of all having control of the city. It means first of all the eviction of the occupiers and the end of occupation so that the people can lead normal lives. Under the abnormal conditions of occupation, we have witnessed in the social areas the things that we have been talking about in all our discussions—expropriation of land and homes, eviction from homes, demolition of homes, wiping out of complete neighbourhoods. All this has social implications for the population. There is forcible transfer of the Palestinian population from inside the city to outside the city and to other areas of the occupied territories and even into the Palestinian diaspora. The enforcement of what is known now as the iron-fist policy by the various Israeli Governments means the impoverishment of the population. It means the present policy of sealing off the occupied territories from East Jerusalem. It impoverishes those workers who work on a daily basis because if they do not work they do not get their salaries, and if they do not get their salaries they cannot make ends meet.

Our colleague Moshe Amirav talked about the map of greater Jerusalem extending from Ramallah to Bethlehem, which would include many Palestinian towns and many more Palestinian villages— which means, for us, more expropriation or confiscation of land, even though he has it in his plan to build housing units in the thousands for Palestinians. I do not know how this is going to be done, because it has to be done on expropriated land.

We are now witnessing a new approach to investment in the occupied territories, which, as mentioned by Mr. Amirav, will entail recycling the taxes to the occupied territories. I think it is indeed the duty of the Israeli Government to do that, because it has been taxing our people for so long without giving them any of the benefits. Our people pay, to the best of my knowledge, about 38 kinds of taxes in the occupied territories. So the social aspect has not been missing, but we have to reread the data that have been given to us today in their social context.

YAEL DAYAN

A confederative solution is almost a gimmick—I am telling you now my private opinion—because Professor Lapidoth will tell you, as will anyone who has a notion of it, that confederation is an agreement between two independent entities on sharing some domains, and it is not a substitute for independence. Now the Labour Party, because it is large and pluralistic, because it is not homogeneous, and for all the good reasons that enabled it to take over and govern, is unable to choose a meaningful and very clear-cut ideology. I see this as a blessing. Some of the results of this lack of clarity are naturally vague definitions that accommodate more than one thing but make progress possible; while the very clear-cut solution may be a dead end. One of these vague solutions offered by the Labour Party is a compromise on a concept that is so far unacceptable to the majority of the Israeli population, including Labour voters—an independent Palestine or, as we say in Hebrew, a third State between Jordan and Israel. For as long as I can remember this has been unmentionable. Nevertheless, the knowledge of many, if not most, of us in the Labour Party is that whatever we are doing now is clearly leading to a two-State solution. I think this compromise was an invention of Foreign Minister [Shimon] Peres, who is very good at things like this which are on the one hand not very clear and on the other really do exclude things that we want to exclude, like annexation or endless autonomy; like saying the unmentionable, a Palestinian State. To my great surprise, this compromise did not create opposition from the other side. So it fell into a sort of niche of acceptance by all sides. King Hussein of Jordan and the PLO leadership did not say, "No way!" to a confederation. So for now, it satisfactorily fills in something that is very difficult to fill in, either by the option of an independent Palestine, which raises concerns from an Israeli point of view, or the Shamir notion of autonomy forever, which is rejected by the Palestinians. The compromise concept is the confederation. I would not exclude it from the jargon of future solutions. As long as it has no opposition there is nothing wrong with it, and perhaps lack of clarity in that phase is something welcome.

As for the future, there *are* blueprints. There are drawn plans, very detailed, and I must mention here that the multilateral working groups of the Madrid Conference are working very actively, and they are producing exactly the body of work that is going to be very satisfactory, I hope, to all sides. It is not only for the post-peace era; it is for the beginning, for the interim arrangement, for self-rule. There are already things that can happen with the cooperation of the entire Arab world, and not just involving the bilateral talks, plus Europe and the United Nations.

ALBERT AGHAZARIAN

Your remarks remind us that the conveners of this Encounter have chosen the theme of "Visions of Reconciliation" deliberately. Perhaps they were afraid that if we started speaking about the social realities of daily life, we would end up either in polemics or in exploding the theme. Neither has occurred, but I think essentially that what we have been saying in this Encounter is that for the past 26 years, Palestinians have been trying to organize, and the Israelis have been trying to disorganize the Palestinians, for the very simple reason that the Israelis did not want a Palestinian State. If the Palestinians succeeded in organizing their infrastructures, their education, and so forth, then eventually they would face a situation where a State becomes inevitable. The Israeli attitude was, anything the Palestinians try to do, disrupt it. Now let us enjoy the wishful thinking or the hope that this has changed, in the sense that perhaps Israel realizes that it would be good to have a Palestinian State. This may be one positive aspect of the brutal closure of the territories. But the sore spot here is the issue of Jerusalem, because this is the connecting line. How can you keep the Palestinian infrastructure developing and ignore the link with its heart, because Jerusalem is certainly the heart, and this is not a spiritual or religious comment—it is a concrete reality. Nothing can physically pass through it, no people can travel through it, no schools can operate. When the occupied territories have been declared closed, no school in Jerusalem can operate and few schools can operate in the West Bank, because a large proportion of teachers and students in the West Bank travel from Jerusalem. In addition, as Mr. Seniora pointed out, many neighbourhoods around Jerusalem are used by Israel as dumping grounds for the extra Palestinian population of Jerusalem. They are technically considered West Bank, and it is easier to build there. But these people depend completely on Jerusalem, and when there is a closure, they cannot come in. It is very complicated, in reality. However, if a decision is made in Israel to have a Palestinian entity, this might bring us to a new orientation. It would be a move away from the classical Israeli position on which there seems to be a consensus in Israel: "no" to a Palestinian State, "no" to what Yael Dayan called a third State between Jordan and Israel.

SARI NUSSEIBEH

I should like to make two points. My first comments have to do with the notion of confederation. Terms in general are set up to communicate ideas and to allow people to understand each other, but very often terms obstruct the transmission of meaning and people get lost while using them. Very often it is not clear to the people concerned what is meant by confederation. So people are either for it or against it just because it is called by that name, and not for any further reason. I think personally that one should look from the bottom up. That is to say, begin with reality rather than with meta-language or whatever, because with reality you have to find exactly what is at stake. What will the Palestinian State need in terms of cooperation and external relations, whether with Israel or with Jordan or Lebanon or Syria or Egypt? Begin from the bottom up and then see how the network of ties is going to be constructed. Where you find that you have reached a level sufficient for your prosperity and progress, there you stop, and you call the network of relations or ties you have established by whatever name you like to give it. It really makes little difference.

The second comment I wanted to make is related to the issue of water and the multilaterals. Ms. Dayan reminded me of something people very often forget about, which is that while you have bilaterals going on, you also have the multilaterals in progress, and although today the bilaterals have begun again in Washington, the other thing that has begun again is the multilateral conference on water. In that multilateral working group as well as in the other multilaterals on economic issues, I think there is a lot of room for developing ideas that directly address regional issues of substance and of cooperation, whether water or resources or economic cooperation. But in our particular meeting here, I think we were more or less required to concentrate our focus on Jerusalem, which is a good thing. By the way, I notice that all the Palestinians in this panel are, in fact, Jerusalemites—Dr. Aghazarian, Dr. Musallam, Mr. Seniora or myself, which is perhaps a coincidence. I believe it isn't.

STEFANOS VALLIANATOS
(Greek Institute of Defence and Foreign Policy)

I am a fellow at the Greek Institute of Defence and Foreign Policy. First, I should like to ask Dr. Lapidoth to comment or give a few more details about the notion of different borders for different functions. How can you separate the activities of people?

Secondly, the Arab-Israeli conflict in general is not only about land or water, or whatever. Israel, some would argue, is a State located in the Middle East that still culturally and politically looks to the West. Even if we reach an agreement on the peace settlement, does that mean that Israel and the Arabs will still simply coexist and that the cultural identity and political affinity of the Israelis towards the West would still be an obstacle to that coexistence? With that in mind, I should like to ask whether in Jerusalem, where people are very near to each other and actually do coexist, the Israelis are creating a kind of new identity, a local identity, rather than a Western-oriented, traditional Israeli identity. Perhaps the immigration of many Russians or other citizens coming to Israel and becoming Israeli citizens is complicating the matter of cultural identity even more.

RUTH LAPIDOTH

I explained earlier that the notion of sovereignty has changed. In this context I also explained that the notion of boundaries has also changed because of very intensive and close communication systems and the ease with which people and information can move across borders. Within the same context, I also mentioned that you can have different boundaries for different purposes. For instance, Geneva is part of Switzerland, but for the purposes of economics and customs duties, there are the free zones around the city which economically belong to Geneva. They do not really "belong" to Geneva, but there are no customs duties when you bring in merchandise and goods from these areas into Geneva. You have other cases where a certain airport is located in a neighbouring country and you have to go through the other country in order to get to that airport. What I am trying to say is that boundaries today are not something so uniform, and you can have different kinds of borders for different purposes, one border for instance for customs duties, and another for strategic matters. As Yael Dayan said, your airplanes may need flyover rights in order to protect both your neighbour and yourself, despite the fact that this airspace may extend beyond your political and economic boundary. It is a complicated system, but I think that it might help to find a solution to specific functions and problems that may arise.

IDITH ZERTAL

Although we Jews come from a hundred places in the Diaspora, from all over the world, I think that we have already developed a very distinctive common identity as Israelis which is very much Mediterranean and Middle Eastern. I would like to remind you that of all the peoples and tribes that have lived in the region over many thousands of years, only the Arabs and the Jews have survived all the generations of invasions, occupations and forced assimilation, and I am sure that both peoples intend to stay there.

RUTH LAPIDOTH

I am sure that once peace is established, there will be much more cultural and social interaction between the two peoples, and I am also sure that this will change the identity of the Israelis. There is no question about that, particularly since about 60 per cent of the Israeli population is originally from Arab countries. I am sure that the strong Western orientation, from a social and cultural point of view, will change with peace.

TOWARDS RECONCILIATION: CONFIDENCE-BUILDING MEASURES

4

PANEL

Moderator
Dr. Sami Musallam
Ms. Yael Dayan
Dr. Idith Zertal

MODERATOR

I hope this Encounter by now has somehow charted a road for us towards some kind of a brighter perspective on things, and that this new outlook can be reinforced by the confidence-building measures that might be suggested by the panellists among us here, particularly those who have some authority to make suggestions either to their Governments or to their organizations, so as to prepare the field for some understanding between the two sides while negotiations are going on. I therefore call again on Dr. Musallam to make his remarks on what kind of confidence-building measures in Jerusalem, in his view, should be carried out so that a solution not only to the Jerusalem issue, but also to the wider problem of the Palestinian-Israeli conflict, can be found one day.

SAMI MUSALLAM

The topic of confidence-building measures is a wide-ranging one and as complicated as the peace process itself. It should go hand in hand with the peace process so as to produce tangible results on the negotiating table as well as on the streets in the occupied territories. And thus the confidence-building measures concerning the city of Jerusalem cannot be separated at all from confidence-building measures concerning the occupied territories as a whole. The major stumbling-block to arriving at peace, a negotiated just peace, is the continuation of the Israeli occupation of the territories, including Jerusalem. To start with, the best kind of confidence-building measure, of course, is to stop the occupation. And then everything would fall into place and peace, a just peace, could be achieved for us and for the Israeli people. But until then, which we hope will be in the very near future because the future of our children and of Israeli children is at stake, if hostilities continue, we should at least start with small steps in the right direction and re-establish or create the confidence that has been lacking in the relationship between the Israeli and the Palestinian people.

I would venture to say that concerning Jerusalem, the first thing for the Israeli Government to do is to stop the iron-fist policy inside the occupied territories as well as inside Jerusalem, because they are closely interrelated. For instance, I don't know the logic behind the fact that when there is a Palestinian demonstration on the streets of Jerusalem or in any town of the West Bank and the Gaza Strip, the Israel Army shoots at the demonstrators. Let them demonstrate. The only thing the Israel Army should do is to withdraw from the scene of the demonstration. In the final analysis, the demonstrators have to go home. And if the Israelis did not shoot at them, there would not be any more escalation that same day. The iron-fist policy is so paramount that it affects every aspect of life in the occupied territories and in Jerusalem. We talked a lot about it yesterday. We have heard Dr. Aghazarian speak emotionally, with facts, about the dramatic oppression to which the Palestinian people are exposed in the Old City of Jerusalem, in the larger area of Jerusalem, as well as in the West Bank. The human rights of the Palestinian people in Jerusalem have to be addressed. Those people should be treated as humans who have their rights in the city of their ancestors where they have been born, where they have lived, where they have been nourished and raised. They need to be able to live their lives as normally as possible in an abnormal situation.

The municipality of Jerusalem is becoming larger and larger. One effective confidence-building measure from the Israeli side would be to re-establish the Arab municipality of Jerusalem which it abolished by decree at the beginning of the occupation of the city in 1967. Israel can do it, without lending any political or ideological undertones to this. This is a measure that has been taken by many Governments or municipalities all over the world when the municipality of a city gets out of hand, when it becomes too large for one administration to handle. The municipality of Tunis has been subdivided in the past three years into three independent municipalities and governments. One governor could not cope with the daily minutiae of the entire greater municipality of Tunis.

Furthermore, since we are talking nowadays of the return of Palestinian deportees, it would be a very good step if the Mayor of Jerusalem, the Mayor of Arab Jerusalem, could be allowed to return. He is in his middle eighties, an old man who has been living for 25 years in exile in Amman, where he had been deported. He should be able to go back and reactivate the frozen City Council of Arab East Jerusalem.

The Israelis should also, as a confidence-building measure, accelerate the process of family reunification as a gesture of good will, because many families are divided on both sides of the border. Or they can create easier conditions, on a daily basis, for people who need permits to leave the country. Take students, for instance: they are given permits to leave for nine months and within those nine months they are not allowed to return, or for two years or three years and they are not allowed to return, allegedly for security reasons. They are allowed to return only after the expiration date of the permit. Israel can alleviate this inconvenience to facilitate people's lives and family reunions for the Palestinian population.

One more important confidence-building measure in Jerusalem would be to guarantee the freedom of worship and access to the Holy Places, which unfortunately, despite Israel's claims to the contrary, is not guaranteed. Recent examples of this are many. Suffice it to say that since Mr. Rabin came to power, the Greek Orthodox Church of the Ascension on the Mount of Olives in Jerusalem was bulldozed by the Israeli occupation authorities. I have the photograph here and I shall pass it to Mr. Tlili to show it around. The bulldozing of the church was done on the pretext that this church had no licence to be built there. For us Palestinians this is really ironic, because the occupation in the first place does not have a licence to occupy our country. Then there is the example which my colleague Dr. Aghazarian mentioned concerning this Easter, when Christian Palestinians from the outskirts of Jerusalem were not allowed to enter Jerusalem for Easter Saturday to receive the holy flame, and to pass it to other Christians in the country. In any event, the Israeli Government and Israeli occupation authorities have failed the test of guaranteeing freedom of access to the Holy Places. There are many examples of desecration of Christian and Muslim Holy Places.

One other measure that would be pertinent to confidence-building in the occupied territories, as well as in Jerusalem, would be to lift the ban on the freedom of movement between the occupied territories and Jerusalem. As was explained earlier, Jerusalem depends on the occupied territories as much as they depend on Jerusalem. If you look at the map displayed here, you see that Jerusalem is in the middle of Palestine, in the middle, so to speak, of the West Bank. If you close Jerusalem to the Palestinians of the occupied territories, then you are really cutting Palestinian communication and free traffic from one part of the occupied territories to the other, because there is no other way than to pass through Jerusalem.

I won't go into the enormous degree of land confiscation, because I have already shown that the Israelis have confiscated one third of the occupied territories to attach it to the greater municipality of Jerusalem. We are not talking about a country as large as Greece or the United States or the Russian Federation. We are talking about mandatory Palestine, and all of it, Israel's and Palestine's area together, is about 27,000 square kilometres. The area of the occupied West Bank is about 5,000 square kilometres and the Gaza Strip is around 280 square kilometres. So we are not talking about large areas. We are really talking about a very, very tiny area. If one third of it has already been confiscated for Jerusalem, the remainder is really minimal, around 4,000 square kilometres, including mountains, rivers, lakes, valleys, townships and agricultural areas. This necessitates fulfilment of the promises made by the Labour Party during the election campaign and on which they have reneged since [Prime Minister] Rabin assumed power, that is, freezing the settlements. Yesterday Yael Dayan said that they have reduced building a lot, almost to the minimum. To the best of my knowledge, we have not witnessed that. She might have better information on that which she can produce and share with us. It is something by which we are obsessed. We are obsessed by settlements, by settlers, day and night, because if you have a piece of land near any settlement in Jerusalem, whether in the area of greater Jerusalem or inside the Old City, or in other parts of the occupied territories, you do not know whether the military authorities will come to confiscate that piece of land and bulldoze your agricultural products and your house. There should be a clear policy in that respect. We know the difficulties that would be faced by any Israeli party or Government that would adopt a clear position of stopping the settlements, because they would have serious opposition from the Right and extremist groups. But we cannot accept that excuse, because what is at stake is our lives and our land and our people. This would be the major confidence-building measure that we expect the Israeli Government to carry out.

The above measures, if adopted, would, to use a Chinese expression, constitute a great leap forward for the peace process. The peace process is stalling, not because there is no desire on our part to achieve peace, but because there are very negligible tangible results on the ground which we can show our people to convince them that the continuation of the peace negotiations is in the interest of the Palestinian people. Nevertheless we are in the peace negotiations because we think they are the way that will lead to a just and comprehensive settlement of the conflict in the very near future. Of course, the Israelis could help a lot with quick movement on the acceptance of the principles of the peace process. This acceptance is not always clear in the public mind, nor even to some political analysts, because one day the Israelis accept the principles on which the peace process is based, and the next day we are not sure. A clear statement by the Israeli Government concerning the applicability of [Security Council] resolution 242 (1967) to the occupied territories including Jerusalem would be a boost for the peace negotiations.

MODERATOR

You made a number of suggestions, Dr. Musallam, regarding the issue of confidence-building measures, which perhaps were heard by the Israeli Government. I hope that our friends in the media listened carefully and will report these suggestions. We shall also hear the other side of the story, and we are blessed to be able to listen next to Ms. Dayan.

YAEL DAYAN

I really have a feeling that we have already covered most issues and that there is very little to add. I am a veteran of discussions of this kind and I feel good about one thing: we have so far engaged in less point-scoring than ever before. Occasionally there has been a below-the-belt accusation, or a turn of phrase that was uncalled for. But on the whole, I feel that we are all maturing in these dialogues by not trying to compete on who killed more, and which people historically suffered more, and who is more evil and who is more democratic, and taking the big picture and cutting it into small visions. If you don't recite this litany, you are often accused of having a heart of stone. I have been accused of not caring. Children are dying in riots, and you are told you don't care. But what is the point of just sitting and equating or balancing the degree of suffering, or trying to draw a symmetry between who is more of a victim? I think those days are over. I think we are all victims equally at different times in history.

I do not accept that all the confidence-building measures should be offered only by one side because there is a victim and a victimizer. There is an occupier and a people that is being occupied and we should be able, maturely and without getting into a big row, to look back a few years and understand the roots of the situation we have now. In 1967, as an Israeli, I was threatened, my survival was threatened. Ten years later my survival was still threatened. Things started changing in 1988. That is just yesterday. It's not historical, it's not the day before yesterday, it's yesterday when I started hearing what a lot of Israelis still have not heard before, and that is a voice of recognition, and something other than a threat to destroy us, to throw us into the sea. I'm not saying this, as you notice, in the tone of a victim. I'm just trying to state that we've got a historical concept about the beginning of the occupation that is not guilt-ridden. We used to wonder whether we were going to be totally thrown into the sea or whether we had to be a fighting nation all our lives and never be accepted in the area. But now, I feel that we have advanced tremendously: we are talking about confidence-building measures for a region where there was no confidence. For decades, for a century, if you wish, it was either us or them. So the fact that we are now talking about whether we will split the area this way or that, whether we will need this or that kind of security guarantee, or how many dunums will be included in Palestine, and whether Israel is going to withdraw from all or just some of the territories is a huge advance which I hope is based on mutual acceptance by the two sides of each other, and acknowledgement of a tragedy for both sides.

Let's face it. Until 1988, Palestinians who talked about partition or compromise were killed for it. Israelis were considered outcasts for the same thing in the prime years of the Likud Administration. Now we've reached a point where there is a majority for a compromise. We've got to nurture this and strengthen it. Both sides have come to terms with reality, and I do not care what the emotion is behind this change. As far as I am concerned, I do not care whether Sari Nusseibeh, deep inside, or Yasser Arafat, deep inside, wants me to disappear from the map. What is important is that they realize that they cannot do it, that I am there to stay. And what is important is that the Israeli people realize that there is a chance for peace, and it has got nothing to do with the territorial compromise, but rather a chance that eventually the Arabs will accept Israel, a Jewish State, in the Middle East, and accept it as there to stay.

So when we talk confidence-building, let us not forget that the idea has a fragile majority at best. Let's first talk about acceptance—accepting the other, which in our case means the Arab world, and the Palestinians and the neighbouring countries doing the same by accepting Israel as there to stay. I hate to think of what we went through during the [Persian] Gulf war. But I know what it did to this confidence-building that we are talking about now. Confidence-building is something mutual even when there is an occupier and an occupied. The occupied still have to contribute to confidence-building, not by, God forbid, really giving something, but by giving the feeling that at the end of occupation there will be a lasting peace, and it will not be just a failed stage towards a revival of the conflict.

We in the peace camp until two years ago were trying to build relationships in spite of all odds, in spite of a Likud Government. We tried to build acceptance for the notion that I, Yael Dayan, can sit with Faisal Husseini, or with Hanan Ashrawi or with Nabil Shaath—sit and talk with the other side in terms of repartition of the area between the Mediterranean and the Jordan River in order to establish a lasting peace forever. And once we establish a border, that's it. It will not be merely a phase, either for Israelis who yearn for a greater Israel, or for Palestinians who dream of turning Israel into part of a secular, democratic greater Palestine. And overnight, because of the Gulf war, the whole thing collapsed. And there I had expected confidence-building from the other side. Not that I had expected them to go against the Arab cause of taking over Kuwait; maybe they think it's something that complies with their notion of independence of countries, although this was horrible for Israel. And not because of the danger of Scuds [missiles], but because of the shattering of our hope that one day we would be accepted by the Palestinians who suffered, who really had a desire to live side by side with us. But there we were: the minute there was again the illusion, the fantasy, someone saying "We'll get you back your Palestine from the Jews and we'll throw them into the sea", there you had rejoicing, the identification with the Iraqis. And this was against the backdrop of the half a million American soldiers. It was lack of realism. Again I'm not speaking about emotions. Maybe it really gave the Palestinians a tremendous boost in the middle of their terrible suffering, and the deprivation and violation of every human right there was in the book, and the despair of listening to the Likud Government, which made it very clear that it was not going to give back an inch of land. But even at the bottom of despair, to fall into the trap of once again relying on the worst of notions, elimination of the State of Israel? I don't know what to say to an Israeli who comes and says to me that there isn't any depth to the Palestinian call for peace on the basis of repartition and a two-State solution. We still have the houses destroyed by the Scuds, we still carry, in this horrible, stupid, idiotic world, our gas masks. Does anyone know what it means for Israel, for all Israelis, to be in sealed rooms with gas masks while Scuds are falling? It wasn't paranoia. The Palestinians were rejoicing. It wasn't a paranoid Jewish desire to be again a victim. It happened, to my great horror. Although not physical horror, because I didn't think Saddam [Hussein] could liberate the Palestinians, Tel Aviv and Jaffa.

Enough therefore of psychology, psychological analysis, when we talk about confidence-building. When I say what I think Israel should be doing, I don't care whether the Palestinians love me or not, whether Mr. Rabin is doing it willingly, or happily, or whether he is going to do it under pressure, as long as he is going to do it, because what is important is the results. And I don't care if [Chairman] Arafat or the PNC [Palestine National Council] express great, deep conviction on getting rid of the paragraph that calls for eliminating the State of Israel. Even if it's *pro forma*, it's enough for me to assure my people.

And I repeat, the same goes for Mr. Rabin. I don't inquire into his deeper feelings. The Labour Government is pluralistic. There are people in the Labour Party, you can quote them, who are committed to peace for territory. In fact, there is no questionthat the entirety of this Government believes this. Some think we should move more slowly, some of them think there are areas we should not give up, but forget about the motivation. The result will be a withdrawal. The result will be confidence, not confidence-building measures. Let's not overemphasize the American invention of confidence-building measures. It depends on what the goal is. Confidence-building in order to reach what? To make sure that autonomy is acceptable to the Palestinians or to perpetuate the majority we both have in our streets? We want the whole thing. Don't give me the icing just so I keep my political majority. Let's regard confidence-building as a means to something, and it should be mutual. We are not Christians, and we are not asking others to be Christians. We don't think of confidence-building as, all right, turn the other cheek. This is not what we have in mind. But when I say, ''Ask for something'', I realize the difficulties. I do not realize them when I think of the Gulf war, but I hope that we have no recurrence of what happened in that war. Many of us have come quite a long way against very difficult odds. You all know about it. Very difficult odds, on both sides. We Israelis cannot give you the keys in our pocket unless we can really promise our people the security of the State of Israel within whatever borders, and you know it and you admit it. But when, after admitting it, we have people like [Ahmed] Jibril [leader of the Popular Front for the Liberation of Palestine—General Command] and [George] Habash [founder and Secretary-General of the Popular Front for the Libera- tion of Palestine], the average Israeli, who is not that sophisticated, listens to them. Now, these people, including Mr. Arafat, all sounded the same five years ago, and I am asking my average Israeli to make a distinction and realize that Arafat is today something else. [Ahmed] Jibril and [Dr. Abdel-Aziz] al-Rantisi [co-founder of Hamas and spokes- man for the deportees of December 1992] are on the other hand still committed to the destruction of the State of Israel. But the aver- age Israeli says that Arafat protects them, and I have to explain on and on . . . .

All I'm saying is that it is not black and white, it's not that sim- ple. So let's engage in confidence-building in a mutual way, and let's see what can happen about stopping or reducing terror. I said be- fore that I personally, and this does not apply to the majority of Is- raelis, do not regard the *intifadah* as anything but resistance. I agree with Sami [Musallam], we should pull out, and this is written in the Washington books already: redeployment of the Israel Army. I hope however that when there is no Israel Army presence, there will be no riots between different groups of Palestinians. We are all afraid of so-called Lebanonization. We are all afraid of the possibility of a vacuum without authority and without force. Let's not be naïve about it, there is this danger. That's why there is a proposal now, not confidence-building, but a security-building proposal, to advance the foundation of the building of a Palestinian police force. We do have a plan for redeployment that is acceptable to the Palestinians, and we're negotiating it now. We can fall into a terrible trap by saying that we can be very generous. But it will not be generosity. We do not want some people, especially on the right, to tell us later, "We told you. We left, and see what happened."

We are building a system that will enable the two sides to enjoy a separation and equality, and eventually a two-State solution, with the least possible interference by Israel in Palestinian life, but enough involvement to strengthen things, so Palestinians can really express themselves in every domain possible during the interim period. We can reach that point in two or three or whatever years, where you are in a position in which your infrastructure is such that you don't really have a problem with assuring security for Israel from terrorism, controlling matters from the inside so we don't have to come in and look for problems. I don't expect the results to be 100 per cent positive, and this is granted, but there must be some confidence-building there too. Seventy per cent of the terrorist acts, and I'm not talking about the *intifadah*, but intentional murders of Jews because they are Jewish, wherever they can be found and with whatever means, still lead back, unfortunately for people like myself, to the PLO. Even Mr. Rabin is not happy about it. I am not point-scoring. I am in a position to sit today at a table and tell you what I can do. I'm not at all powerful. Israel is a democracy. The Labour coalition has a small majority. I'm not hiding behind it. But you've got to accept it. It's a very fragile majority and unless confidence is coming from the other side as well, we are going to lose this majority and I don't want even to think where we will all end up. If [the] Labour [Party] is not in Government, we can sit forever with United Nations decisions and claim we must do thus and so, and try to impose it on Israel. Believe me, it's almost impossible. Mr. Rabin has a wonderful obsession about the importance of the United States—let's use it. Mr. Shamir had the opposite. He wanted to show that we can stand against the whole world because we are right, but he was so wrong, which made him even more determined. He's got, like many on the right, like many of the Shiites, like many of the terrorists in any religion, a suicidal tendency. Mr. Shamir was suicidal for the entire State of Israel. They've got what we call the Masada complex. We'll stay put, we'll be suicidal, but we will establish our independence of mind, and independence and superiority of ideology. I don't want to be a Masada. I don't want the Palestinians to be an Arab Masada. I don't want to go down in the hero's books. I want to be alive. I want my grandchildren to live and not to have to serve in the army. I believe that you people want the same.

Yesterday, in Washington, D.C., there was a long list of things that had been requested before, and not given, or took a long time to be given. Some of the things on this list were published and some were not, I believe, although we will hear from the Palestinians at the end of every day that no progress was made. It's perhaps part of the strategy or tactics. [Mr.] Arafat was very optimistic yesterday, but the spokespeople for the delegation were less optimistic. On that list are basic things. Let's all grab them. I usually don't say this any more to Palestinians, because they get so offended. To them, it sounds condescending. I say, "Let us together grab the opportunity." When I say it's the only game in town, I'm not saying it to be superior. For me it *is* the only game in town. I'm not saying to you, "Come on, guys, come play this game because we will not offer you another game." I don't have another game. I cannot get peace for my people unless I play this game. And this includes offering control of two thirds of State land, the inverse of previous offers. And this includes a larger council, and major legislative rights, not only administrative, and not only by-laws, but in all domains other than those that presuppose sovereignty, like foreign affairs and defence. It includes a large police force to be trained immediately now. It includes elections. We all know what elections mean. Elections are the best possible political exposition of independence. This slogan is on bumper stickers everywhere, and balloons. It's Arafat buttons and somebody else's buttons. It's loudspeakers. It's saying loud and clear the word Palestine. The Palestinians are being offered elections under any supervision they want, in whatever system they want, for a council that will be larger than the one originally proposed. I say, "Yes, grab it, because you are democratic. You're going to be, after Israel, only the second democratic society and country and State in the Middle East." We can't impose a curfew on you when you are having elections. Hopefully, those who object to a peace process and elections will not jeopardize them by terrorizing you and us at the same time. But this is something that can be done immediately.

There is talk about a variety of human rights. However much we do is of course not enough. I know that this has the sound of confidence-building if we, as we announced yesterday, are going to bring back deportees who were deported long ago. At first there was a list of 35. I believe there will be lists like this on a weekly basis. Detainees are going to be liberated. You can say this is nothing. It is *not* nothing. It cannot be done all at once, not until the Palestinian flag flies above. I do not think it will fly over Jerusalem in the first go. Maybe if, that is, you know, if this will be your final condition and you will say, "Either Palestine with Jerusalem, or no Palestine." I agree with all the proposed separate municipal arrangements and free access from the territories to Jerusalem. All this will lead one day to a flag flying over somewhere, which will be the centre of an independent Palestine.

All the rest is not enough, granted. So if we let out 1,000 detainees, and you say this is nothing, that's not what I mean by confidence-building from your side. If you say this is nothing, the average Israeli says, "Well, if they don't appreciate it anyway, why should we free some people who have been caught in active terrorism one way or another? If nothing is enough for them, a Palestine will not be enough for them either." I don't say you have to accept gracefully. Accept with clenched fists and grind your teeth and complain, but don't underestimate the difficulty in carrying out even what you call totally unimportant gestures. Because the next day, and it happened a few weeks ago, there may be a stabbing at the bus station.

I have not managed so far to explain to the average Israeli the difference between Sari Nusseibeh and the man with the knife who goes into a high school and just stabs to kill, knowing he will be caught. You've got explanations for it. But what motivates the mother of the child who gets stabbed? There isn't an explanation. There isn't an explanation because otherwise this world will be an impossible place to live in. There isn't an explanation. There is no justification. And there should be a law above it all, for a Palestinian who stabs and for an Israeli who does things not according to the law, and we've got them in prison. And that's talking about confidence-building. We ourselves have soldiers in prison. We've got settlers in prison, for shooting when they are not in life-threatening danger. We've also got cases every day for which there is no excuse. Give us at least credit for being some kind of democratic, law-abiding country, because if I can't walk away with this, none of us have got anything. I will end here.

Everyone can read in the papers what is happening in Washington. I hope both sides really grasp the opportunity with the basic confidence that we mean a solution that will end occupation and get Israel, excuse me, the hell out of the territories—not all of them as I said, most of them. And we will live side by side and this will be it. Not as a first stage and not as a third stage towards a fourth one. This will be it and then we'll start confidence-building, because now there is too much hate, too much animosity, too much suffering and too much pain without sort of weighing who has got more. We'll build the confidence the minute we are separated, as odd as it may sound. Because I don't know of a confidence that is imposed by an occupier. Occupation in itself is a negation of anything to do with confidence. Terrorism in itself is a negation of anything to do with confidence. So let's separate first and then build our confidence.

I should like to thank Mr. Tlili, on behalf of our delegation, for having given us the chance to appear here on the same day that the negotiations restarted, which I think fills our souls with a degree of optimism.

MODERATOR

You know very well, Yael Dayan, that I have always admired your eloquence and your courage, and this is what we need in the situation now prevailing in the Middle East. We need eloquence to express what cannot be expressed in formal negotiations, because this is what we need to achieve between the two sides: a real dialogue—and this dialogue of course sometimes requires eloquence, frankness and sincerity. We also need courage. Courage is required, but it is lacking in the Middle East. The courage to go beyond formal, known positions and to reach out to the other side. This is why, when we drafted this programme, we did not think of confidence-building measures as an end in themselves, but as an avenue towards reconciliation between Palestinians and Israelis, leading to a lasting, just and comprehensive peace. This is how the United Nations envisages it, and what Secretary-General Boutros Boutros-Ghali has called for repeatedly over the past two years. This is the only chance that the area has, and that is why both the General Assembly and the Security Council, and also the Secretary-General, have given their full support to the peace process going on in Washington. We are of course gratified that on the day we meet here, that peace process is resuming in Washington.

IDITH ZERTAL

Before I go wandering in other provinces, as I admit I cannot add much to the concrete issues that have been dealt with in the past day and a half, I shall try to enlarge a little upon our concepts. But before I do that, let me start with a personal remark. I wish Yael Dayan was in a much more influential, policy-making position in Israel. Let's not be fooled. She needs all the fighting spirit you have experienced here, and her eloquence, to pave her way in Israeli politics, within Israeli society and within her own political party. Her positions and opinions are not so obvious in Israel yet. I hope they will be in the near future, but for the moment, she needs all the support the people of my milieu in Israel can give her, and I thank her for her positions uttered here with such eloquence, as has been said.

Now I should like to use the time allotted me to deal with two maybe quite philosophical concepts of history, and especially of historical rights, because I think that the concept of historical rights is one of the major obstacles towards reconciliation in our region, and I think it applies to all of us here on both sides. We all have problems born out of what we call historical rights. I do not deal with history because I am nostalgic about the past. I am a historian by formation, but I am sure we can draw some lesson from history for the present, and for the immediate future. So let's look at the ravages that this quite abstract concept of historical rights causes all over the world. Tribes, peoples, nations, are butchering, destroying each other, in the name of historical rights. We talked earlier about the fundamentalist Muslims and of the danger Islamic extremism represents for the region, for the whole world. We Jews in Israel have our own fundamentalists, and they are extremists no less than the Islamic ones. They are not religious by definition, but they use the Bible and the Holy Scriptures for their current political purposes. They use them quite selectively, to be sure. They find there, in the Bible, a licence to confiscate, to expel, to transfer, even to kill.

"Historical rights" is the magic phrase for those who deny political rights to the Palestinians. We are the lords of the land, they say. Greater Israel was given to us, to the Jewish people, by God himself and therefore it is not in the hands of human beings, and it is absolutely forbidden to give away even a small part of it to strangers. What is meant by historical rights? For whom? So-called historical rights are a very tricky business. It is usually the aspirations and the political ambitions of the present that shape what is called historical rights. People old enough will find in distant history any cover, any explanation, any justification for whatever political claims they may make, and in contradiction to other people's claims. In most of the cases, the historical rights of one people do not make room for the historical rights of another people. Some say that there is no such thing as objective, measurable historical rights. Who can judge which historical rights are older, more sacred, stronger or morally valid? Where is the international body or the providential authority to do that? Will military might decide it? In our case, how can one decide who is the real owner of the land? The one that was expelled from the land 2,000 years ago and loved it from afar, and prayed for it, and sang songs about it and felt like a foreigner everywhere else, or the one who lived on the same land for centuries without interruption, cultivated a house on it and raised his family there? Could such a people be expelled just because you yourself were once expelled from this land? Jews have a historical link to the entirety of Palestine, but so do the Arabs. In Hebron are buried the fathers of the Jewish nation. But on the other hand, Jaffa was once a very important political and cultural Arab centre. Jerusalem, it has been repeatedly mentioned, is holy for the Jews. There stood the First and the Second Temples. But Jerusalem is no less sacred for the Muslims and the Christians, so it is crucial to understand the difference between affinities and historical memories, attaching a group of people to a place where it once lived and giving rise to claims by that group to have absolute and exclusive rights to that place in the present. The only human solution to conflicting claims is sharing, division, partition, a political solution to a political situation. And the land is a land is a land. Let's not forget that land is divisible. We are not facing a Solomon's trial kind of a case. We are not talking about cutting children into two, only a piece of land. And as has already been said, Israel is strong enough, in my view, to defend itself in its previous frontiers, which gave it, by the way, much more security than the present frontiers.

Now to history. In my view, history is mostly interpretative. It is in the eye of the beholder, in the mind of the beholder. There is no one linear, objective, absolute history. There is no one history but many histories. The same historical facts are regarded and interpreted differently by different people in different times. Let's take the example of the establishment of the State of Israel. In Jewish eyes, it is seen as a kind of modern miracle, an age-old dream come true. But for the Palestinians, it is a real tragedy, and we the Jews have to admit it. What we Jews consider as the Zionist solution to the Jewish question is in fact the birth of the Palestinian question. There is an overweight of history and memories in our region. History, or so-called history, is used and abused time and again on both sides. The history of the region is a history of suffering, loss and pain. We Israelis have just come out from the most painful week in our calendar. The week that begins with Holocaust Day goes on to Remembrance Day for the Fallen Soldiers in Israel's Wars, and ends with Independence Day. This is the week we count and mourn our dead, and there are so many of them. The Palestinians also have their martyrology. They are in the process of creating their national calendar, and it is full of the dead and the martyred. Every other day they have a strike or remembrance ceremony for one martyr or another. That is how a people creates its national identity. This is the process. We know it. We have done the same.

The question is, what does one do with one's suffering? How does one capitalize on it in one's life? Groups, as much as individuals, use past and present sufferings to legitimize their current demands.

There is much capital in suffering. The world prefers the victims, even if it doesn't help them much. Indeed, it seems all too easy to have every political argument resolved by someone referring to his or her own, or to the group's, suffering. Suffering can be instrumentalized and harnessed for evil goals. It can be abused as a warrant for all kinds of oppression towards others. It can also be harnessed to positive purposes. Suffering and pain do not always make one just and noble. Very often, they distort our perception of the world and of history and our conduct. What is needed now is not a fight over history, history revisited, but politics achieved. Not remembrance and nostalgia for old times, but real action on the ground. Both parties to the conflict are not going to evaporate. The Palestinians cannot extract us from the region. We cannot occupy and abuse them forever. What is needed now is a revolution in the minds, a total change in mutual images, in the image of the other.

I should like to finish my very short exposé with a poem written by a well-known Israeli poet, a Jerusalemite named Yehuda Amichaï. The poem, in my translation, goes like this:

> From the place where we are right,
> There will never grow
> Flowers in the spring.
>
> The place where we are right
> Is dry and hard
> Like a yard.
>
> But doubts and loves
> Liven the earth
> Like a mole, like a plough.
> And a whisper will be heard in the place
> Where stood the house
> That was destroyed.

So let's not destroy our houses.

FLOOR DISCUSSION

Mr. Antonis Economides	Dr. Sami Musallam
Dr. Albert Aghazarian	Dr. Idith Zertal
Dr. Ruth Lapidoth	Mr. Hanna Seniora
Ms. Yael Dayan	

MODERATOR

I now open the floor for discussion. Again, I should like to invite our friends in the media to address as many questions as they wish, either to the panel collectively or to one of the panellists more specifically.

ANTONIS ECONOMIDES *(To Vima)*

We have heard many interesting things yesterday and today and we thank you. I should like to request, however, a particular statistical bit of information which I did not hear. Would it be possible to know the area of Jerusalem, its population and the breakdown into Jewish and Muslim populations? Of course, I know it would not be easy to give me these numbers because we would have to go back to the census of 1915 or perhaps to 1947 and 1967, or today's. But I should be grateful for a bit of enlightenment regarding this as well as the results of polls in Jerusalem as to what exactly the people want for the future. The question is directed to whomever would like to answer it.

MODERATOR

Dr. Aghazarian, you might wish to answer the first part of the question and then we shall see who would like to answer the second part of the question on public opinion.

ALBERT AGHAZARIAN

Statistics in the case of Jerusalem are very political. Jordanian Jerusalem, that is, Jerusalem in 1967, was 1,500 hectares. Now an additional 6,000 hectares of land has expanded the metropolitan area. The plan that Mr. Amirav was presenting for metropolitan Jerusalem, which is still not finally approved but is in an advanced phase, would have 10 more square miles, which means covering the entire region between Ramallah and Bethlehem. One of the most interesting things about this demographic distribution is that very important neighbourhoods of Jerusalem have been excluded from the official map of the city. For example, you have neighbourhoods around Jerusalem, such as A-Ram and Abu Dis, where you have 50,000 to 60,000 people. They are the dumping grounds for excess Jerusalemites. The Israeli press has carried stories clearly indicating that the Government has informed the municipality that the policy guideline should be that under no circumstances would Arabs be more than one third of the total population. This is the Government's position. The second governmental guideline is to have a majority of Jews in eastern, occupied Jerusalem. Right now we have an estimated 130,000 settlers living in occupied East Jerusalem, and about 150,000 Arabs. This means you have no less than 100,000 people who are for all intents and purposes Jerusalemites, who have been flushed out into neighbourhoods that, according to paperwork, are considered part of the West Bank. And so these people have no right of access to Jerusalem.

Another point, technical in appearance: in 1968 the Israelis conducted a census of the population. They wanted simply to count the people who were there in the area. This was done in a direct form. Curfews were imposed everywhere, and statisticians came and checked who was there. Based on this census, people were forced to take Israeli identity cards. In the case of Jerusalem, they were issued by the Ministry of the Interior, since Jerusalem is supposedly part of Israel. In the case of the West Bank, they were issued by the Israel Army. This was over and above the Jordanian passport which the original population was holding in 1967. This technical-looking administrative operation juridically transformed the status of the entire Palestinian population, in one package, from citizens into residents, which means green-card holders, if we want to use the American model. Juridically, any Palestinian, including Jerusalemites, is considered a resident. If I am out of Jerusalem, the city of my birth, for more than one year, then juridically speaking I am a Jordanian. There is no distinction between me and someone living in Amman all his life. If I have property, my property will be considered absentee property. These are, I think, technical matters which are extremely important.

When we travel, these details are important—we apply for a laissez-passer, a permit to travel. This laissez-passer is issued by the Israeli Ministry of the Interior and in it, it says "Citizenship, Jordanian". This travel document is for one year and you need a visa everywhere you go because it says "Citizenship, Jordanian". Now I, as a so-called Jordanian citizen, am not allowed to stay more than one month in Jordan. When I have to fill out a form at the hotel, or if I want to rent a car, there is a line indicating citizenship. Each time, I face a problem because if I put Palestinian, it's as though I'm making a dangerous political declaration. If I put that I am an Israeli, I am being an impostor. If I put that I am a Jordanian, Jordan is not my country. When I happened to be on the plane to Madrid, they gave us the landing card. It said "Citizenship", and this was the first time that, with excitement, I have written, "To be determined in Madrid". Even with my children, the same problem. People ask them what their flag is. If the children tell them the Palestinian flag, they could get arrested. The whole situation is an aberration, and no matter how much we want to philosophize, it requires change.

Another issue is the zoning areas. From 1967 until now, not a single Arab housing project of any relative substance was approved in East Jerusalem. Not a single one. There was talk that the Arabs need 25,000 apartments from now until the year 2004. Then the figure went down to 12,000. Then it went down to 7,000. Finally we hear that there is a final approval of 6,000 residential units, collective housing units. We don't know where the area would be. What will happen? Which area? It's on paper, and it's like a fantasy.

I want to make one additional point here. On Saturday, 24 April, just the day before I left for Athens, at 10 o'clock in the morning at the gate of my university, out of nowhere, a roadblock was placed. Soldiers stopped, they piled up stones and started blocking cars. This was not a normal roadblock. It accumulated, I can assure you, no less than 80 cars in each direction, at the gate of the campus. I am often involved in talking to the military in cases like this to help defuse things. I walked out to the patrol and said, "Listen, we've had an extended meeting with ex-Minister [Moshe] Arens about this matter. We have had meetings with the head of the Civil Administration and the Military Governor of Ramallah, and they have assured us that they will avoid provocations like this." The officer I talk to tells me, "Talk to them. I don't receive my orders from you or from them. I have instructions to do it and I am going to do it." I tell him that he's harassing the whole campus, impeding classes and people. He says that he's outside the campus. But he was literally at the gate of the university. When you try to reach officials, they tell you no one is there. This is Saturday and no one is there. Or on another day when you ask for a certain officer with whom you have contact, the secretary tells you, "One minute, let me see if he is around." He is not around. This is on a day-to-day basis. When I come back from a conference like this, my students will say, "They are at it again, at the gate of the university." What can you do about it? And it is an 18-year-old soldier who tells you, "Move, these are my instructions. Get the hell out of here."

So when we speak of confidence-building measures, it is not something that is theoretical. It is not a question of feelings. It is not a question of different attitudes and history and so on. We are speaking about concrete, day-to-day issues. We are speaking about a situation where I personally, on a daily basis, have to assist no less than 800 faculty members to get to the campus because they are from Hebron and they are from Bethlehem and they are from Gaza, and these people simply have to come in order to study or to teach. Now we still haven't dealt with the student aspect of the matter, how to get them to campus in view of the closure order. This is between Hebron, between Bethlehem, between Ramallah and Bir Zeit. You talk to Israeli officials, and everything is nice. "No problem", they say. "We are not going to block education. Just send us a fax with all the names you need." We send a fax and then the next day the people in Bethlehem get the permission, all of them. The people in Hebron, for some reason or other, do not get it. The people in Gaza, half of them get it after waiting six hours and the other half don't. So they come, they get the permission, and it's for one week. After one week we have to start all over again. And after one week you try to find the original officer with whom you have struck the deal, and he is not around. This is our life on a day-to-day basis. It's a question of harassment, and I shouldn't complain because the bulk of the population has to stand for hours and hours and hours for the most petty operation. Imagine the extremes I have to go to in order to get permission for our architecture students to visit the Dome of the Rock to see an example of Umayyad or Mamluk construction. This is why people in the final analysis are becoming very sceptical about the negotiating process, because what they need is concrete, day-to-day kinds of things. These are points that I feel are important to underscore in order to move away from the spectrum of schematic and long-range thinking and into the daily life of Palestinians.

MODERATOR
I understand that Dr. Lapidoth would like to say a few words on the question of polls and public opinion.

RUTH LAPIDOTH

Actually it is not on that question that I should like to speak because I did not bring the numbers with me. So if you are interested, please leave me your address and when I get home, because we have a statistical yearbook, I shall be happy to send you the numbers that you were asking for.

My second remark concerns the issue of citizenship of people in East Jerusalem. When the unification of Jerusalem took place in 1967, Israel changed its nationality law and gave the residents of East Jerusalem the option to have Israeli nationality. Unfortunately, most of the residents of East Jerusalem preferred not to become Israeli nationals.

YAEL DAYAN

I think for the sake of all peace-seekers and -lovers, it's better not to poll public opinion in Jerusalem about the future of Jerusalem. I do not mean to imply that Jerusalem people are different in their morals or in their deeper concepts, but Jerusalem is a right-wing city. It's got a large population of religious and orthodox people.

We conduct national polls on every issue, including Jerusalem. We do not consider the Jerusalemites separately because they are not going to make decisions on their city on their own. Count on it, this decision is of course a national one. The only measuring stick we've got is elections, because with elections we can distinguish how many votes went to each party and each ideology and in which geographical place. [The] Labour [Party] does not have a majority in Jerusalem. This applies to the Knesset elections, where ideological issues do come up. We do have a Labour Mayor of Jerusalem, fortunately, but this is largely because of his personal appeal, and he is a very moderate person. I have doubts as to how long he will continue as Mayor simply because of his age. He is 82. I would dare to say that in the municipal elections that are to be held in November 1993, there is a good chance that a Likud person will take over, which will just add to the problems. But political decisions on Jerusalem are made in the Knesset, and we will have for a while a Labour Government with perhaps a Likud mayor of Jerusalem. A separate poll on Jerusalem, in Jerusalem, is like asking the settlers what they think about the future frontiers of the State of Israel. All you really need to do is look at the results of the last election.

SAMI MUSALLAM

I do not want to be sarcastic, but Professor Lapidoth portrayed the Israeli offer of citizenship as some kind of magnanimous offer by the Israeli Government which we nasty Palestinians rejected. Well, first of all, it was, and is, occupation by a third country of our land; secondly, it was annexation of Jerusalem; and thirdly, it was an imposition of a third nationality on us. We are Palestinians. We are neither Israelis, nor Jordanians, nor Greeks for that matter, nor any other nationality. Why should we change our nationality? It is for the Israelis officially to recognize Palestinian nationality.

YAEL DAYAN

When we talk about settlements and confidence-building, we should be clear about the differences between the present Government and the previous one. The first decision of the Labour Government was to stop building any new settlements. This is not completely satisfactory because this Government is committed to a certain number of units already started, although that number has been inflated. The fact is that the Government is not building [new settlements]. There are a certain number of houses that are really there already and have to be completed because of contracts with contractors. The Government simply cannot afford to pay these contracts, so therefore it allows a certain number of units to continue to be built. The good news is that there isn't a line of people who are waiting for these houses to be completed so they can move there to live. There is an evacuation of places. But the question is that in the end it is not so much the number of units. We have to understand one thing. The previous Government tried to do something irreversible and offered heaven and earth to whomever would settle. The settlements did not appeal to Russian immigrants, because they did not like everything that went with that, other than the economic benefits. We stopped all additional economic benefits and we reduced existing ones, including education and the financing of certain defence needs. The Government has removed all its subsidies, which were enormous, from the entire settler population, and this I think is very courageous. Economically speaking, it had been very tempting to move to the West Bank and live there, and now it has become not only not tempting, but you would have to be crazy to move there. Whether it is roads, communications or education, the whole system that the Likud created on the West Bank, which was subsidized, is now over. From the economic standpoint, people have gone to look for jobs beyond the green line and commute back home, and many of them are trying to sell their houses. But Israelis do not stand in line to buy houses in settlements, and you can see every Friday in the advertisements the number of houses for sale in the West Bank and in the [Gaza] Strip.

ALBERT AGHAZARIAN

I have one point of clarification on what Dr. Musallam said. In fact we do not have a Palestinian nationality. We have a Palestinian identity. Technically speaking, we have no nationality whatsoever. That is my first remark. Secondly, with reference to what Professor Lapidoth said, some years ago a fellow panellist here, Dr. Nusseibeh, suggested that maybe we should all apply for Israeli citizenship, all the people in the occupied territories. Why don't we become Israelis and play the game within the State of Israel? The response was, in Labour circles especially, that this would be the most dangerous way to destroy the Hebrew State. Very clearly, both the Likud and Labour [Parties] were not excited about the idea. And just theoretically, if someone wanted to organize a campaign in East Jerusalem for all of us to get Israeli passports, I can assure you that this would be rejected by the authorities and there would be methods to foil the attempt, rather than accept, say, 150,000 or 180,000 additional Arabs in the State. I mean the general attitude is that there are already too many Israeli Arabs, about 800,000.

IDITH ZERTAL

I wanted just to add a remark to what Yael Dayan has said about the settlements. There is a joke going around in Israel, and it asks why the Palestinian construction workers are so happy building the houses in the settlements, and the answer is that they are building their own future homes. I am sure that in the final agreement, the Palestinians will get the houses in the settlements from which we Jews will withdraw. Don't you worry, Dr. Aghazarian, you are constructing your own houses.

HANNA SENIORA

I should like to refocus on the subject of the day: how we can attempt to build the future in Jerusalem. I want to comment that certainly these small steps that we are anticipating would change the trends that have been imposed on us for the past 26 years of occupation. And one of the trends is that we have not been allowed housing in Jerusalem. You look at the map showing the green area. If this green area became yellow, then we could create more housing. There is one place to the south of Jerusalem, near Bethlehem, where today Israel is attempting to create a new neighbourhood, called Arnona. If we want to show that Jerusalem will be the city of peace and coexistence, instead of planning a Jewish neighbourhood to change the demography of East Jerusalem, a Palestinian neighbourhood could be built in its place, and this would immediately send a signal that possibly there could be an understanding over the issue of Jerusalem.

My second remark touches upon an issue that Dr. Musallam this morning elaborated on as a confidence-building measure. The Mayor of Arab East Jerusalem, Mr. Khatibi, was expelled 26 years ago. He is mentioned as one of the figures that might be allowed to return in the next few weeks, hopefully even earlier. Now the intention on the Palestinian side, and I think it is going to happen very soon, is that, as Israel unilaterally annexed our part of the city and unilaterally closed our municipality, we will now unilaterally declare that this municipality is being revived, with or without its head, Mr. Khatibi. We hope that it will become operational. Certainly such a municipality will have a planning committee, and we would like to envigorate it by having younger people, because many officials of this municipality are old. Dr. Musallam mentioned that Mr. Khatibi, our Mayor, is more than 80 years old. He is probably the same age as Teddy Kollek. We would like to have new, younger people participating in the municipality of East Jerusalem. Another idea that was mentioned was to set up neighbourhood councils. We would like, and I think we are going, in the future, to set up neighbourhood councils, separate from the Israeli councils, which would be connected to the municipality of East Jerusalem.

MODERATOR

I should like to inform you that Dr. Musallam has requested me to tell you that on his identity card, delivered by the Tunisian authorities because he lives in Tunisia, he is listed as Palestinian, and that for his nationality he is listed as Palestinian, and for his place of birth, Jerusalem is noted.

SUMMATIONS AND CONCLUSIONS

5

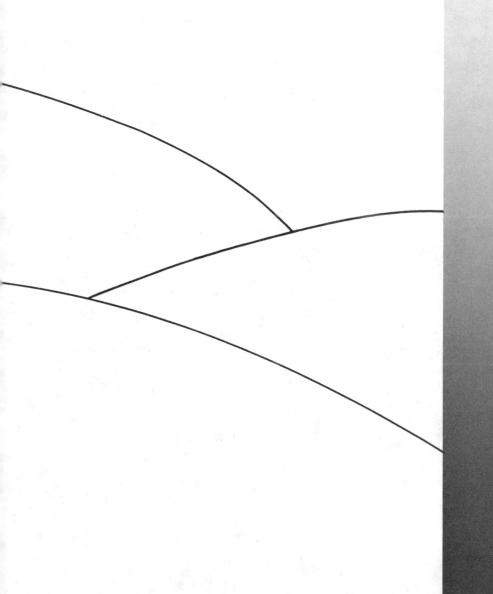

PANEL[*]

Ambassador Robert V. Keeley
Mr. Valery I. Kuzmin

ROBERT V. KEELEY

On behalf of all of the participants here, I should like to thank the sponsors, the United Nations most of all and its Department of Public Information, for arranging this Encounter, and the Ministry of Foreign Affairs of Greece, the Athens Daily Newspaper Publishers' Association and the Grande Bretagne Hotel for providing the venue. I think I can speak for all of us in saying that we have enjoyed the Encounter. In my case, I have spent as much time and energy giving interviews and talking to the press as I have contributing to this meeting from this platform. I think that is all part of the reason for this kind of meeting. The informal exchanges we have had during the breaks and after the close of proceedings have been extremely valuable—I hope for you, as much as for us.

I shall not try to summarize all the points of view that have been expressed here. I have to start with a caveat by saying that the conclusions I have drawn are personal views. I am not trying to speak for the whole group. What I think I have learned is that the issue of Jerusalem is just as difficult as we always thought it was, and yet I do not believe it is insoluble. I think there is a solution. I think that with good will, it can be worked out and it has to be worked out between the two parties directly involved. I furthermore believe that it is an issue that should be addressed now rather than later. It would be a mistake to leave it for another three to five years. I have said this before, and what has been discussed here has simply confirmed that view in my mind. If it is put off that long, the issue may become insoluble. It needs to be addressed now as part of the current negotiations on autonomy. Furthermore, finding a solution for Jerusalem could show the way for a solution to the éntire problem. As I tried to point out at the beginning, I do not think that the issues differ in kind, but only in degree and in the amount of emotion involved.

There seems to be agreement that the city should remain undivided, that is, unified or united. That is a beginning, because that

---

[*] In addition to the two members of this panel, Dr. Sami Musallam and Dr. Sari Nusseibeh took the floor for brief comments.

has certain implications that are inescapable. If you are living in one city, you have to learn how to live together with others, and that means you have to learn how to make compromises. The most difficult issue is the one of sovereignty, but I think a contribution was made towards that. It seems to me that the consensus is that since there is not going to be a division physically of the city, sovereignty has to be joined or dual, or shared, or whatever term one chooses to use, although normally sovereignty is not something you share. A country, a government, a person, is sovereign. In a given locality, territory or piece of land, that sovereignty cannot normally be shared with anyone else. What this requires of us is a bit of imagination. I do not see why sovereignty cannot be shared. Why does it have to be exclusive? Why cannot it be inclusive? Why not just finesse the issue and say we are not going to get into an argument about sovereignty, we are both sovereign here, and then deal with the problems that are caused by living in the same city? As some of the panellists said, it is a question of how you divide up the functions, not how you divide up the territory.

John Whitbeck, an American international lawyer living and working in Paris whose hobby, if that's the right term, for the past five years has been trying to solve the Israeli-Palestinian issue, has drafted a paper in which he attacks Jerusalem head-on. He, like some of the rest of us, is of the opinion that it has to be part of the solution and in fact has to be central to it. Here is what he writes:

"The status of Jerusalem poses the toughest problem for any settlement plan causing many to assume, for this reason alone, that no settlement acceptable to both sides can ever be reached. When the United Nations General Assembly adopted resolution 181 (II) in 1947, it addressed the problem by suggesting an international status for Jerusalem with neither the Jewish nor the Arab State to have sovereignty over the city. Yet joint undivided sovereignty, while rare, is not without precedent. Chandigarh is the joint undivided capital of two Indian States. For more than 70 years, the entire Pacific State of Vanuatu, formerly the New Hebrides, was under the joint undivided sovereignty of Britain and France. For more than 700 years, the Principality of Andorra has been under the joint undivided sovereignty of French and Spanish individuals, currently the President of the French Republic and the Bishop of Seo de Urgel, while its administration is entrusted to an elected general council. Until German reunification, the western sectors of Berlin under American, British and French sovereignty were jointly administered by an autonomous elected senate. As a joint capital, Jerusalem could have Israeli Government offices, principally in its western sector; Palestinian Government offices, principally in its eastern sector; and municipal offices in both. A system of districts or French-style *arrondissements* could bring municipal government closer to the different communities in the city. To the extent that either State may wish to control persons or goods passing into it from the other State, this could be done at the points of exit from, rather than the points of entry into, Jerusalem. In a context of peace, particularly one coupled with economic union, the need for such controls would be minimal. In a sense, Jerusalem can be viewed as a cake, which could be sliced either vertically or horizontally. Either way, the Palestinians would get half the cake. But while most Israelis could never voluntarily swallow a vertical slice, they might just be able to swallow a horizontal slice. Indeed, by doing so, Israel would finally achieve international recognition of Jerusalem as its capital. Jerusalem is both a municipality on the ground and a symbol in the hearts and minds. Undivided but shared in this way, Jerusalem could be a symbol of reconciliation and hope for Jews, Muslims, Christians, and the world as a whole."

Mr. Whitbeck came to this metaphor of the cake by first thinking of the city as a pie. A pie gets sliced up into triangular pieces and if you hand one slice to somebody and they eat it, it's gone. The other person has lost it. So he said why don't we rebake that thing and make it a layer cake. Two layers with a lot of icing on them for Yael Dayan, who mentioned icing earlier. There is a Palestinian layer and there is an Israeli layer and you don't cut the cake at all. You keep it whole. In other words, you have your cake and you eat it too.

MODERATOR

Before I give the floor to Mr. Kuzmin for his summation, Dr. Musallam has asked for the floor for a minute or two to make a remark.

SAMI MUSALLAM

My remark concerns what Ambassador Keeley just mentioned: he felt that there is general agreement that Jerusalem should remain united or unified. I cannot let such a statement pass without comment, because it warrants clarification. I have said, yesterday and today, that our position, and my personal position as well, is that [Security Council] resolution 242 (1967) applies to Jerusalem, East

Arab Jerusalem, inasmuch as it applies to the other occupied territories; i.e., East Jerusalem is part and parcel of the territories occupied by Israel since 1967.

VALERY I. KUZMIN

I should like to make some personal observations and remarks on the course of our Encounter. To my mind, this day and a half of discussion as a whole has been positive and useful, though only time and, in particular, the productivity of the ongoing peace process will show whether it can be instrumental in future formal talks on the issue of Jerusalem. I am glad to state that some of my opening remarks are similar to the opinions expressed here and are even very much in tune with some of the closing remarks of the esteemed Mr. Keeley. To my best judgement, the general balance of all the presentations made by the parties directly involved is still slightly in favour of emotion and divergence rather than cold-minded scrutiny and practical tackling of the issue. It is only natural and explicable given the history of their relations and the recent escalation of tensions in the West Bank, including East Jerusalem and especially Gaza. Still, we got together to talk peace, and we did so trying to find some common denominators that could be useful in the perspective of an overall settlement. With this said, we should of course bear in mind the extreme diversity of the matters and facts involved, the mosaic of reality on the ground so emphatically shown by Dr. Aghazarian.

Permit me to concentrate on the points of importance for the further job of negotiating a settlement, I mean an Arab-Israeli settlement as a whole, and a solution for this particular problem as a part of it. The main presentation of Ms. Dayan stressed the fact that the present Israeli Government as well as public opinion are not yet ready to seek a practical compromise on Jerusalem. From her words, though, it is implicitly clear that the process of thinking about the previously unthinkable has already started. May I share the view of Mr. Amirav and others who pointed out the predominantly psychological character of this process? Both sides are very much aware of the danger that extremists could take the upper hand in the battle for the minds of the rank and file among the Palestinians and the Israelis. In this regard, the negotiating approach of Dr. Nusseibeh seems to me very attractive and encouraging. All of us, the parties directly involved in the peace process and the international community including the United Nations, must remember and take the practical steps arising from the fact that the present historic chance for peace is unique and should not be lost.

At the same time, I can hardly agree with some ideas, such as, for example, that the rise of Islamic fundamentalism in the occupied territories is mainly the problem of Palestinians or that it can be discounted and brushed away as a general phenomenon of the Arab and Muslim world. In this particular case, the roots are evident and result primarily from the occupation and the human suffering caused by it, though some external factors are involved too.

Before proceeding to the identification of the points which to my mind enjoy the majority support of the panellists, I should like to emphasize the undeniable need for scrupulously keeping the balance in tackling any of the issues involved, for example, in drawing parallels between such issues as human rights abuses against Palestinian civilians and security concerns of Israel. Israelis are entitled to security, there is no doubt about it, but as an occupying Power for more than a quarter of a century, Israel is supposed to bear the major share of responsibility for the state of affairs in the territories which it controls. This is true not only from the points of view of international law, United Nations legality and new values of the post–cold war world, but from the economic, social and maybe moral standpoint.

Now I am going to tell you what is in common, what are the convergences found in the presentations, though of course, maybe not all the panellists will agree with my opinion.

The first point is that there is a well-recognized right of both parties to Jerusalem and more or less recognition of the applicability of the principle of land for peace or, in a broader sense, the principle of compromise while settling these controversial and contradicting claims.

The second point is the undesirability from many points of view of a new partition, physically, of the city; preferably, its open character would be kept from outside as well as from inside. There is an agreement about the need for free access to the Holy Places for all the interested religions and denominations, including, in the first place, of course, the population of the nearby West Bank and other Palestinian territories. It was also suggested, and there were no open objections to this idea, that there may be established some kind of a supervising, maybe extraterritorial, body to oversee the arrangements related to free access to the Holy Places. There is a need for some mechanism of arbitration between the major communities in the city.

As for sovereignty, it seems to me that most of us prefer a mixed model for splitting or sharing both political and economic sovereignty over the city.

There is also a kind of consensus on preserving mutual interest in the day-to-day programmes, plans and municipal development of the city, not only in its present borders, but in the suburbs that are also involved in its life. The most desirable would be the greatest possible degree of demilitarization and restriction or minimization of the exercise of force, or any arbitrary actions or violent harassment of the communities or their representatives in the city. There is a need for abstention from physical and demographic changes, at least without mutual consent of the main parties involved. Whether you call it confidence-building measures or any other name, I suppose that is not the point. The point is that, in this regard, I join Dr. Zertal in calling for real action on the ground.

In conclusion, may I appeal once more for patience, mutual acceptance and a thorough scrutiny of all the chances available for addressing the issues with less emotion and more reason.

MODERATOR

Dr. Nusseibeh has asked for the floor for a few comments, which I hope will be brief, as we have limitations on our time.

SARI NUSSEIBEH

I wish to make two criticisms of the Encounter. One is that I felt that we did not really focus on the issue for which we have been brought to Athens, which is Jerusalem. Much of the discussion was about the general political problem, sometimes using language that was verging towards rhetoric. I thought this was not really very useful. I can mention examples on both sides.

The second remark I wish to make is that I felt in particular that our Israeli colleagues on the panel have not addressed the issue of Jerusalem at all, if I make a comparison between how the Palestinian side and even the non-Palestinians were talking about the issue and what our Israeli colleagues have had to offer. We on the Palestinian side focused on Jerusalem, whether in terms of confidence-building measures or in terms of possible solutions, or in terms of problems that we suffer as Jerusalemites and as Palestinians, whereas on the whole, unfortunately, on the Israeli side I did not hear a reciprocity in focus. I hope that this was not intended.

MODERATOR

I take note of your comments. I hope that in the future we will be able to focus a little bit more on the issue that we debate.

CLOSING REMARKS

6

CLOSING REMARKS

Moderator

MODERATOR

The time has come to conclude this Encounter. I have been impressed with the quality of these discussions, which have been spirited and informative. While it is clear that a variety of different views were expressed by the panellists, with some of you coming from fundamentally different directions, it is equally clear that all of you here on the panel share a solid commitment to arriving at a workable common ground. I believe this Encounter offers evidence that the issue of Jerusalem can indeed be addressed in a way which could lead to a solution that is just and satisfying to both Palestinians and Israelis. We were aware, at the United Nations, that tackling the issue of Jerusalem might be a difficult task. We were also aware that we would be entering uncharted waters. We put our faith, however, in the capacity of the distinguished women and men at this table to believe in the superiority of dialogue over any obstacles that can separate people. It seems, and I hope you would agree with me, that our faith was vindicated.

The contribution of our invited senior media representatives and other experts has been invaluable in this endeavour by eliciting additional commentary and analysis from the political and intellectual members of the panel. We at the United Nations attach great importance to public opinion, especially as it impacts on the question of Palestine. We recognize that no real peace can be achieved or sustained without the informed support of the general public— Palestinian, Israeli, Arab and international.

Therefore I extend my sincere appreciation to all participants, distinguished panellists, media representatives and others for contributing to this priceless goal of reconciliation on the issue of Jerusalem.

I also should like to thank the Athens Daily Newspaper Publishers' Association for helping to make possible our stay at this lovely hotel, the Grande Bretagne, whose staff and facilities have been so helpful to our discussions.

I have only admiration for the interpreters who have rendered our lively discussions into both Greek and English.

We most especially owe a great debt to the staff of the United Nations Information Centre at Athens. Without the valuable contribution made by the Director of the Centre, my colleague Mr. Axel Wuestenhagen, this Encounter would not have been possible. Sadly for many of us here and for many of you in Athens, he departs for a new post in a few short days. In your name, in my name and in the name of my colleagues, I should like to wish him every success and much happiness as Director of the United Nations Information Service at Vienna.

We have been overwhelmed by the generosity of the Greek Government, whose support has been unstinting and its hospitality lavish. On behalf of the United Nations and the Secretary-General, I should like to express my special appreciation and gratitude to the Greek Government and particularly to the Minister for Foreign Affairs of Greece, His Excellency Mr. Michael Papaconstantinou, whose auspicious opening of this Encounter launched these important discussions.

Finally, I wish to reiterate my sincere thanks and appreciation to the panellists assembled here, whose collective experience, expertise and wisdom have contributed to these valuable discussions. I wish each of you Godspeed on your journey home, or wherever your efforts for peace may take you.

To conclude, I should simply like to let you know that we in the Department of Public Information will continue our Encounters between Israelis, Palestinians, members of the media and other experts. We shall meet in London in June 1993 to continue the dialogue on the question of Palestine.

GENERAL ASSEMBLY RESOLUTION 181 (II)
[EXCERPT]

Adopted on 29 November 1947
Future government of Palestine

PLAN OF PARTITION WITH ECONOMIC UNION

PART I. Future constitution and government of Palestine

. . .

PART II. Boundaries

. . .

C. THE CITY OF JERUSALEM

The boundaries of the City of Jerusalem are as defined in the recommendations on the City of Jerusalem. (See Part III, Section B, below.)

PART III. City of Jerusalem

A. SPECIAL RÉGIME

The City of Jerusalem shall be established as a *corpus separatum* under a special international régime and shall be administered by the United Nations. The Trusteeship Council shall be designated to discharge the responsibilities of the Administering Authority on behalf of the United Nations.

B. BOUNDARIES OF THE CITY

The City of Jerusalem shall include the present municipality of Jerusalem plus the surrounding villages and towns, the most eastern of which shall be Abu Dis; the most southern, Bethlehem; the most western, Ein Karim (including also the built-up area of Motsa); and the most northern Shu'fat, as indicated on the attached sketch-map.*

---

* See annex III, City of Jerusalem: Boundaries Proposed by the Ad Hoc Committee on the Palestinian Question.

C. STATUTE OF THE CITY

The Trusteeship Council shall, within five months of the approval of the present plan, elaborate and approve a detailed Statute of the City which shall contain *inter alia* the substance of the following provisions:

1. *Government machinery; special objectives*

The Administering Authority in discharging its administrative obligations shall pursue the following special objectives:

a) To protect and to preserve the unique spiritual and religious interests located in the city of the three great monotheistic faiths throughout the world, Christian, Jewish and Moslem; to this end to ensure that order and peace, and especially religious peace, reign in Jerusalem;

b) To foster cooperation among all the inhabitants of the city in their own interests as well as in order to encourage and support the peaceful development of the mutual relations between the two Palestinian peoples throughout the Holy Land; to promote the security, wellbeing and any constructive measures of development of the residents, having regard to the special circumstances and customs of the various peoples and communities.

2. *Governor and administrative staff*

A Governor of the City of Jerusalem shall be appointed by the Trusteeship Council and shall be responsible to it. He shall be selected on the basis of special qualifications and without regard to nationality. He shall not, however, be a citizen of either State in Palestine.

The Governor shall represent the United Nations in the City and shall exercise on their behalf all powers of administration, including the conduct of external affairs. He shall be assisted by an administrative staff classed as international officers in the meaning of Article 100 of the Charter and chosen whenever practicable from the residents of the city and of the rest of Palestine on a non-discriminatory basis. A detailed plan for the organization of the administration of the city shall be submitted by the Governor to the Trusteeship Council and duly approved by it.

3. *Local autonomy*

a) The existing local autonomous units in the territory of the city (villages, townships and municipalities) shall enjoy wide powers of local government and administration.

b) The Governor shall study and submit for the consideration and decision of the Trusteeship Council a plan for the establishment of special town units consisting, respectively, of the Jewish and Arab sections of new Jerusalem. The new town units shall continue to form part of the present municipality of Jerusalem.

4. Security measures

a) The City of Jerusalem shall be demilitarized; its neutrality shall be declared and preserved, and no para-military formations, exercises or activities shall be permitted within its borders.

b) Should the administration of the City of Jerusalem be seriously obstructed or prevented by the non-co-operation or interference of one or more sections of the population, the Governor shall have authority to take such measures as may be necessary to restore the effective functioning of the administration.

c) To assist in the maintenance of internal law and order and especially for the protection of the Holy Places and religious buildings and sites in the city, the Governor shall organize a special police force of adequate strength, the members of which shall be recruited outside of Palestine. The Governor shall be empowered to direct such budgetary provision as may be necessary for the maintenance of this force.

5. Legislative organization

A Legislative Council, elected by adult residents of the city irrespective of nationality on the basis of universal and secret suffrage and proportional representation, shall have powers of legislation and taxation. No legislative measures shall, however, conflict or interfere with the provisions which will be set forth in the Statute of the City, nor shall any law, regulation, or official action prevail over them. The Statute shall grant to the Governor a right of vetoing bills inconsistent with the provisions referred to in the preceding sentence. It shall also empower him to promulgate temporary ordinances in case the Council fails to adopt in time a bill deemed essential to the normal functioning of the administration.

6. Administration of justice

The Statute shall provide for the establishment of an independent judiciary system, including a court of appeal. All the inhabitants of the City shall be subject to it.

7. *Economic union and economic regime*

The City of Jerusalem shall be included in the Economic Union of Palestine and be bound by all stipulations of the undertaking and of any treaties issued therefrom, as well as by the decisions of the Joint Economic Board. The headquarters of the Economic Board shall be established in the territory of the City.

The Statute shall provide for the regulation of economic matters not falling within the régime of the Economic Union, on the basis of equal treatment and non-discrimination for all Members of the United Nations and their nationals.

8. *Freedom of transit and visit; control of residents*

Subject to considerations of security, and of economic welfare as determined by the Governor under the directions of the Trusteeship Council, freedom of entry into, and residence within, the borders of the City shall be guaranteed for the residents or citizens of the Arab and Jewish States. Immigration into, and residence within, the borders of the city for nationals of other States shall be controlled by the Governor under the directions of the Trusteeship Council.

9. *Relations with the Arab and Jewish States*

Representatives of the Arab and Jewish States shall be accredited to the Governor of the City and charged with the protection of the interests of their States and nationals in connection with the international administration of the City.

10. *Official languages*

Arabic and Hebrew shall be the official languages of the city. This will not preclude the adoption of one or more additional working languages, as may be required.

11. *Citizenship*

All the residents shall become *ipso facto* citizens of the City of Jerusalem unless they opt for citizenship of the State of which they have been citizens or, if Arabs or Jews, have filed notice of intention to become citizens of the Arab or Jewish State respectively, according to part I, section B, paragraph 9, of this plan.

The Trusteeship Council shall make arrangements for consular protection of the citizens of the City outside its territory.

12. *Freedoms of citizens*

a) Subject only to the requirements of public order and morals, the inhabitants of the City shall be ensured the enjoyment of human rights and fundamental freedoms, including freedom of conscience, religion and worship, language, education, speech and Press, assembly and association, and petition.

b)　No discrimination of any kind shall be made between the inhabitants on the grounds of race, religion, language or sex.

c)　All persons within the City shall be entitled to equal protection of the laws.

d)　The family law and personal status of the various persons and communities and their religious interests, including endowments, shall be respected.

e)　Except as may be required for the maintenance of public order and good government, no measure shall be taken to obstruct or interfere with the enterprise of religious or charitable bodies of all faiths or to discriminate against any representative or member of these bodies on the ground of his religion or nationality.

f)　The City shall ensure adequate primary and secondary education for the Arab and Jewish communities respectively, in their own languages and in accordance with their cultural traditions.

The right of each community to maintain its own schools for the education of its own members in its own language, while conforming to such educational requirements of a general nature as the City may impose, shall not be denied or impaired. Foreign educational establishments shall continue their activity on the basis of their existing rights.

g)　No restriction shall be imposed on the free use by any inhabitant of the City of any language in private intercourse, in commerce, in religion, in the Press or in publications of any kind, or at public meetings.

13.　Holy Places
a)　Existing rights in respect of Holy Places and religious buildings or sites shall not be denied or impaired.

b)　Free access to the Holy Places and religious buildings or sites and the free exercise of worship shall be secured in conformity with existing rights and subject to the requirements of public order and decorum.

c) Holy Places and religious buildings or sites shall be preserved. No act shall be permitted which may in any way impair their sacred character. If at any time it appears to the Governor that any particular Holy Place, religious building or site is in need of urgent repair, the Governor may call upon the community or communities concerned to carry out such repair. The Governor may carry it out himself at the expense of the community or communities concerned if no action is taken within a reasonable time.

d) No taxation shall be levied in respect of any Holy Place, religious building or site which was exempt from taxation on the date of the creation of the City. No change in the incidence of such taxation shall be made which would either discriminate between the owners or occupiers of Holy Places, religious buildings or sites, or would place such owners or occupiers in a position less favourable in relation to the general incidence of taxation than existed at the time of the adoption of the Assembly's recommendations.

14. *Special powers of the Governor in respect of the Holy Places, religious buildings and sites in the City and in any part of Palestine*
a) The protection of the Holy Places, religious buildings and sites located in the City of Jerusalem shall be a special concern of the Governor.

b) With relation to such places, buildings and sites in Palestine outside the city, the Governor shall determine, on the ground of powers granted to him by the Constitutions of both States, whether the provisions of the Constitutions of the Arab and Jewish States in Palestine dealing therewith and the religious rights appertaining thereto are being properly applied and respected.

c) The Governor shall also be empowered to make decisions on the basis of existing rights in cases of disputes which may arise between the different religious communities or the rites of a religious community in respect of the Holy Places, religious buildings and sites in any part of Palestine.

In this task he may be assisted by a consultative council of representatives of different denominations acting in an advisory capacity.

D. DURATION OF THE SPECIAL RÉGIME
The Statute elaborated by the Trusteeship Council on the aforementioned principles shall come into force not later than 1 October 1948. It shall remain in force in the first instance for a period of ten years,

unless the Trusteeship Council finds it necessary to undertake a re-examination of these provisions at an earlier date. After the expiration of this period the whole scheme shall be subject to re-examination by the Trusteeship Council in the light of the experience acquired with its functioning. The residents of the City shall be then free to express by means of a referendum their wishes as to possible modifications of the régime of the City.

Security Council Resolution 242 (1967)

Adopted on 22 November 1967

The Security Council,

Expressing its continuing concern with the grave situation in the Middle East,

Emphasizing the inadmissibility of the acquisition of territory by war and the need to work for a just and lasting peace in which every State in the area can live in security,

Emphasizing further that all Member States in their acceptance of the Charter of the United Nations have undertaken a commitment to act in accordance with Article 2 of the Charter,

1. *Affirms* that the fulfilment of Charter principles requires the establishment of a just and lasting peace in the Middle East which should include the application of both the following principles:

i) Withdrawal of Israel armed forces from territories occupied in the recent conflict;

ii) Termination of all claims or states of belligerency and respect for and acknowledgement of the sovereignty, territorial integrity and political independence of every State in the area and their right to live in peace within secure and recognized boundaries free from threats or acts of force;

2. *Affirms further* the necessity

a) For guaranteeing freedom of navigation through international waterways in the area;

b) For achieving a just settlement of the refugee problem;

c) For guaranteeing the territorial inviolability and political independence of every State in the area, through measures including the establishment of demilitarized zones;

3. *Requests* the Secretary-General to designate a Special Representative to proceed to the Middle East to establish and maintain contacts with the States concerned in order to promote agreement and assist efforts to achieve a peaceful and accepted settlement in accordance with the provisions and principles in this resolution;

4. *Requests* the Secretary-General to report to the Security Council on the progress of the efforts of the Special Representative as soon as possible.

Security Council Resolution 338 (1973)

Adopted on 22 October 1973

The Security Council

1.   *Calls upon* all parties to the present fighting to cease all firing and terminate all military activity immediately, no later than 12 hours after the moment of the adoption of this decision, in the positions they now occupy;

2.   *Calls upon* the parties concerned to start immediately after the cease-fire the implementation of Security Council resolution 242 (1967) in all of its parts;

3.   *Decides* that, immediately and concurrently with the cease-fire, negotiations shall start between the parties concerned under appropriate auspices aimed at establishing a just and durable peace in the Middle East.

GENERAL ASSEMBLY RESOLUTION 47/64 C

Adopted on 11 December 1992
Question of Palestine

The General Assembly,

Having considered the report of the Committee on the Exercise of the Inalienable Rights of the Palestinian People,[a]

Taking note, in particular, of the information contained in paragraphs 66 to 84 of that report,

Recalling its resolutions 46/74 C and 46/75 of 11 December 1991,

Convinced that the world-wide dissemination of accurate and comprehensive information and the role of non-governmental organizations and institutions remain of vital importance in heightening awareness of and support for the inalienable rights of the Palestinian people,

1. *Takes note with appreciation* of the action taken by the Department of Public Information of the Secretariat in compliance with General Assembly resolution 46/74 C;

2. *Requests* the Department of Public Information, in full cooperation and coordination with the Committee on the Exercise of the Inalienable Rights of the Palestinian People, to continue, with the necessary flexibility as may be required by developments affecting the question of Palestine, its special information programme on the question of Palestine for the biennium 1992-1993, with particular emphasis on public opinion in Europe and North America and, in particular:

a) To disseminate information on all the activities of the United Nations system relating to the question of Palestine, including reports of the work carried out by the relevant United Nations organs;

---

[a] *Official Records of the General Assembly, Forty-seventh Session, Supplement No. 35 (A/47/35).*

b) To continue to issue and update publications on the various aspects of the question of Palestine, including Israeli violations of the human rights of the Palestinian people and other Arab inhabitants of the occupied territories as reported by the relevant United Nations organs;

c) To expand its audiovisual material on the question of Palestine, including the production of such material;

d) To organize and promote fact-finding news missions for journalists to the area, including the occupied territories;

e) To organize international, regional and national encounters for journalists.

MAPS

UN PARTITION PLAN—1947
AND
UN ARMISTICE LINES—1949

—··—··— Boundary of Former Palestine Mandate

PLAN OF PARTITION, 1947

Arab State

Jewish State

Jerusalem

- - - - Armistice Demarcation lines, 1949
(Shown where at variance with Mandate boundary.)

MEDITERRANEAN

SEA

SINAI

EGYPT

LEBANON

SYRIA

GOLAN

Lake
Tiberias

WEST

BANK

Jordan

Amman

JORDAN

Dead
Sea

ISRAEL

GAZA

Tyre
Quneitra
Nahariyya
Acre
Safad
Haifa
Shef ar'am
Tiberias
Nazareth
Nawa
Hadera
Jenin
Netanya
Tulkarm
Kefar Sava
Qalqilya
Nablus
Tel Aviv
Arab
Jaffa
Rishon Le Zion
Ramle
Ramallah
Jericho
Rehovot
Latrun
Jerusalem
Bethlehem
Hebron
Gaza
Khan Yunis
Rafah
Beersheba
El Arish

Elat

Gulf of
Aqaba

ISRAEL

LEBANON

SYRIA

Tel Aviv

Jerusalem

JORDAN

EGYPT

The designations employed and the presentation of
material on this map do not imply the expression of
any opinion whatsoever on the part of the Secretariat
of the United Nations concerning the legal status of
any country, territory, city or area or of its authorities, or
concerning the delimitation of its frontiers or boundaries.

MAP NO. 3067   UNITED NATIONS
SEPTEMBER 1979

CITY OF JERUSALEM
BOUNDARIES PROPOSED
BY THE AD HOC COMMITTEE
ON THE PALESTINIAN QUESTION

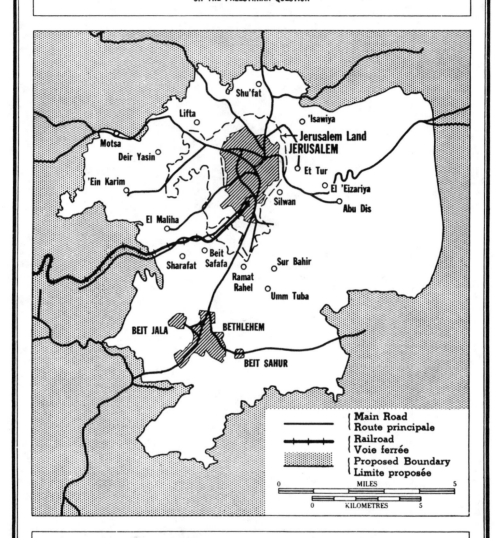

Shu'fat

Lifta

'Isawiya

Motsa

Deir Yasin

Jerusalem Land
JERUSALEM

Et Tur

'Ein Karim

El 'Eizariya

Silwan

Abu Dis

El Maliha

Beit
Safafa

Sur Bahir

Sharafat

Ramat
Rahel

Umm Tuba

BEIT JALA

BETHLEHEM

BEIT SAHUR

Main Road
Route principale
Railroad
Voie ferrée
Proposed Boundary
Limite proposée

0   MILES   5

0   KILOMETRES   5

VILLE DE JERUSALEM
LIMITES PROPOSEES
PAR LA COMMISSION AD HOC
CHARGEE DE LA QUESTION PALESTINIENNE

TERRITORIES OCCUPIED
BY ISRAEL
SINCE JUNE 1967

MEDITERRANEAN
SEA

LEBANON

GOLAN

Quneitra

Nahariyya

Nawa

SYRIAN ARAB
REPUBLIC

Haifa

Tiberias

Nazareth

Jenin

Netanya

Tulkarm

Nablus

Qalqilya

Tel Aviv

WEST BANK

Jordan

Amman

Ramle

Jericho

Jerusalem

Bethlehem

Hebron

Dead
Sea

Gaza

GAZA

JORDAN

Rafah

Bersheeba

ISRAEL

EGYPT

SINAI

— — — Armistice Demarcation
Line, 1949

—··—··— Boundary of Former
Palestine Mandate

The designations employed and the
presentation of material on this map do
not imply the expression of any opinion
whatsoever on the part of the Secretariat of
the United Nations concerning the legal status
of any country, territory, city or area or of its
authorities or concerning the delimitation of its
frontiers or boundaries.

Elat

0 10 20 30 40 km

0   10   20   30 mi

MAP NO. 3243 Rev.3   UNITED NATIONS
AUGUST 1993

141

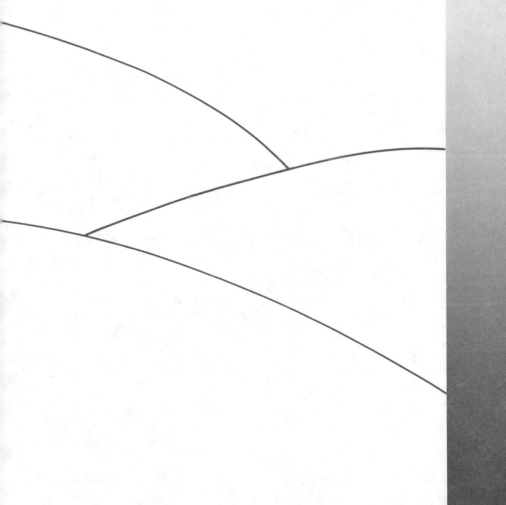

Blueprint for Jerusalem

Moshe Amirav

For years, the subject of Jerusalem has been a nightmare for anyone interested in Arab-Israeli peace. Scores of solutions have been proposed, but none offered an end to the old zero-sum game: any gain for one side meant an unbearable concession for the other. The issue seemed best put off until it became unavoidable. But now it is on the agenda for the Israeli-Palestinian talks. A new approach is needed that can defuse the issue of sovereignty — what state Jerusalem will belong to — and offer gains to both sides.

For the past year, Hanna Siniora, editor of the East Jerusalem daily Al-Fajr, and I have initiated discussions here and abroad on this challenge. Among the participants have been high PLO officials and Israeli intellectuals and politicians. Based on those talks, Siniora and I drafted a blueprint for Jerusalem's future; because influential figures from both sides have contributed, we believe this is the first plan with a strong chance of being politically acceptable to Israel and the Palestinians.

We propose redrawing the city's boundaries to quadruple the current land area, adding an almost equal amount of territory from Israel and the West Bank. The Palestinian towns of Ramallah and Bethlehem would be included, along with the Israeli suburb of Mevasseret Tzion and the West Bank settlement of Ma'aleh Adumim. With the new boundaries, the metropolitan area would have about 450,000 residents of each nationality, creating parity that could be maintained in the future and ending the 80-year battle for demographic advantage. The Arab gain of parity would be matched with legitimacy for Jewish suburbs and neighborhoods beyond the pre-67 borders.

The entire area, we suggest, would be under the jurisdiction of a Greater Jerusalem Council. Under that roof body, the metropolis would be divided into 20 cities, each with its own municipal government. On both levels, local government would have far more power than it currently does in Israel. Today, cities get most of their funds from the national government; they do not control planning, schools or police within their boundaries; decisions often must be approved by government ministries. We propose transferring many of these functions to the metropolitan council and the cities. Within their boundaries, they'd control education, health services, courts, planning and development, and would collect taxes besides the existing property tax to pay their own bills.

In principle, the Jewish cities would be under Israeli sovereignty; the Palestinian ones would belong to a Palestinian state, or in an initial stage to the Palestinian autonomous authority in the West Bank. Jerusalem would serve as the capital of both states. But because the role of central governments in the metropolis itself would be vastly reduced, so would the importance of sovereignty. Functionally, Jerusalem would be an autonomous unit, in which Jews and Arabs would live together and share power equally. Rather than struggling endlessly for supremacy, Arabs and Jews would have a framework for cooperation, a framework that would produce a new mind-set and create a model for peace.

Israelis in Jerusalem would be citizens of Israel. They'd live in Israeli cities, and vote for Israeli mayors and city councils. The Palestinians, likewise, would live in Palestinian municipalities and be citizens of a Palestinian state. The metropolitan council would be joint Israeli-Palestinian, with delegates from each city and a rotating chairperson. Holy places would be managed by a body made up of delegates from all three faiths.

Because of the particular sensitivity of the Old City, it would have its own municipal government, with both the Israeli and Palestinian governments having veto power over any changes in the status quo, and with representatives of the three religions on the city council.

This plan offers not only political but major economic benefits. The metropolis would have land resources that today's city desperately lacks. New land will provide space for developing industry and housing for both Arabs and Jews. Peace and security will further encourage growth, attracting investments from around the world and providing new sources of employment. New jobs will stop the exodus of those in search of work, now nearly 10,000 a year. A city of peace will attract centers of culture, education, religion, new museums and new universities. And new economic opportunities will help raise the Arab standard of living to that of Jews, removing another source of conflict in the City of Peace.

The plan, at first glance, would require Israel to give up half its rule of Jerusalem. In fact, it would gain rule over more land because of the expanded borders. Israel would also achieve, for the first time, world recognition of its status in the city. And it would reap economic benefits, security and peace. The Palestinians, too, can only gain from this concept.

Without a solution for Jerusalem, there can be no solution to the Arab-Israeli conflict. Instead of dodging the issue, then, why not put it at the top of the negotiating agenda? Under the plan proposed here, Jerusalem would become an example of partnership that would alter attitudes among Israelis and Palestinians alike, and make further steps toward peace easier. In particular, success in Jerusalem would make Israelis more open to the idea of a Palestinian state.

Once we create peace and justice in Jerusalem, the rest will fall into place. ❑

Moshe Amirav, a former Likud activist, now represents Shinui on the Jerusalem City Council and heads the council's committee on East Jerusalem affairs.

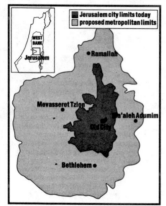

Jerusalem city limits today / proposed metropolitan limits

WEST BANK • Jerusalem • Ramallah • Mevasseret Tzion • Ma'aleh Adumim • Old City • Bethlehem

MAP OF JERUSALEM

SUPPLIED BY MR. HANNA SENIORA

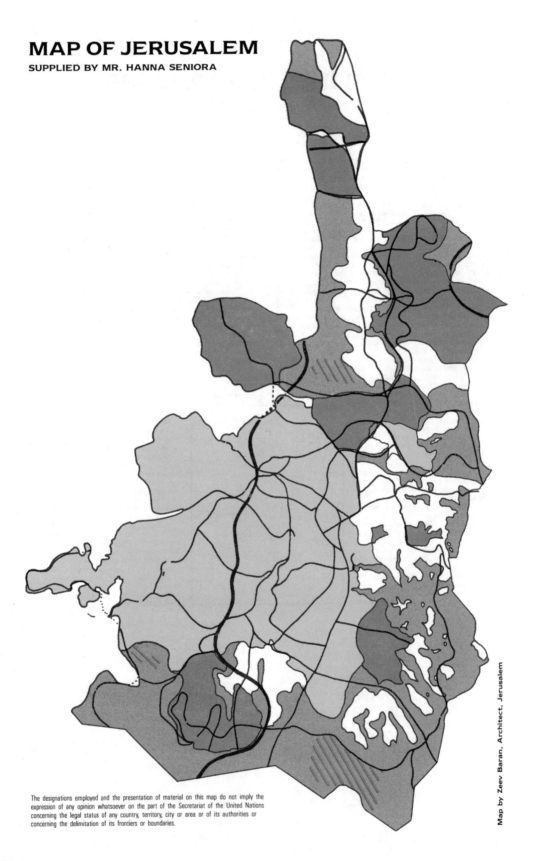

The designations employed and the presentation of material on this map do not imply the expression of any opinion whatsoever on the part of the Secretariat of the United Nations concerning the legal status of any country, territory, city or area or of its authorities or concerning the delimitation of its frontiers or boundaries.

Map by Zeev Baran, Architect, Jerusalem

'Down from the bottom is the south of Jerusalem, near the Bethlehem area. The upper side is towards Ramallah, which is the north of Jerusalem. The lighter pink area is West Jerusalem and you can see the old green line dividing East Jerusalem and West Jerusalem. The darker pink areas are the new "facts on the ground" that have been created by the Israelis since 1967. Almost 50,000 dunums have been expropriated from East Jerusalem and the West Bank to create new "facts". Before 1967 no Israeli lived in East Jerusalem. Today in 1992 we have 130,000 Israelis living in East Jerusalem and we have about 160,000 Palestinians living there. In the next two years when the 60,000 housing units that Israelis are building in East Jerusalem and the surroundings have been completed, we, the Palestinians in East Jerusalem, will become a minority in our part of the city. The yellow areas[1] are the remaining ghettos of East Jerusalem surrounded by the pink areas and what is called green land.[2] Green land represents the areas where Palestinians are forbidden to build. They are zoned as a green area theoretically for public use, but "public use" in the Israeli dictionary means that these areas will next be incorporated into the Israeli part of Jerusalem when Israel has digested what it has already taken. If you look at the southern part of the city, there is an area which is green with pink stripes. This is an area where Israel is trying to build another new neighbourhood. There is also in this green area farther to the west another place, near Walajah, where Israel is also trying to build another area, and in the northern part of the city near Shafad there is another part of the green area where Israel is building new "facts on the ground".'

Mr. Hanna Seniora (see p. 69)

---

[1] Shown as white on the facing map.
[2] Shown as grey on the facing map.